The **AA** P[...]

PRAGUE

Prague: Regions and Best places to see

Original text by Christopher and Melanie Rice
Updated by Heather Maher

© Automobile Association Developments Limited 2008
First published 2008

ISBN: 978-0-7495-5529-0

Published by AA Publishing, a trading name of Automobile Association Developments
Limited, whose registered office is Fanum House, Basing View, Basingstoke,
Hampshire RG21 4EA. Registered number 1878835.

Colour separation: Keenes, Andover
Printed and bound in Italy by Printer Trento S.r.l.

Front cover images: (t) AA/C Sawyer; (b) AA/J Smith
Back cover image: AA/J Smith

A03404
Maps in this title produced from mapping © MAIRDUMONT / Falk Verlag 2007

About this book

Symbols are used to denote the following categories:

- map reference
- address or location
- telephone number
- opening times
- restaurant or café on premises or nearby
- nearest underground train station
- nearest tram route
- nearest overground train station
- nearest ferry stop
- nearest airport
- admission charge
- other places of interest nearby
- other practical information
- ▶ indicates the page where you will find a fuller description

This book is divided into five sections.

Planning pages 6–19
Before You Go; Getting There; Getting Around; Being There

Best places to see pages 20–41
The unmissable highlights of any visit to Prague

Exploring pages 42–107
The best places to visit in Prague, organized by area

Excursions pages 108–127
Places to visit out of town

Maps pages 131–144
All map references are to the atlas section. For example, Karlův most has the reference ✚ 134 D2 – indicating the grid square in which it is to be found

Contents

Planning

RANSKÁ

Before You Go

WHEN TO GO

JAN	FEB	MAR	APR	MAY	JUN	JUL	AUG	SEP	OCT	NOV	DEC
-1°C	0°C	4°C	9°C	14°C	17°C	19°C	18°C	14°C	9°C	4°C	0°C
30°F	32°F	39°F	48°F	57°F	63°F	66°F	65°F	57°F	48°F	39°F	32°F

🔵 High season 🔵 Low season

Temperatures are the **average daily maximum** for each month.

Prague has hot summers and bitterly cold winters. May and June and then September and October are the best times to go, although Prague's winter snow can be great, with the concert and opera seasons at their height. Go in spring to see the wonderful show of blossoms on the fruit trees of Petřín Hill and avoid the oppressive heat of summer. However, January to March, and November are the best times to go if you want to avoid the hustle and bustle of tourist crowds.

Autumn is a lovely time to visit when the days are still bright with sunshine but the crowds have dwindled. Come in freezing winter to visit the markets and join the New Years' crowds in the streets.

WHAT YOU NEED

- ● Required
- ○ Suggested
- ▲ Not required

Some countries require a passport to remain valid for a minimum period (usually at least six months) beyond the date of entry – check before you travel.

	UK	Germany	USA	Netherlands	Spain
Passport/National Identity Card	●	●	●	●	●
Visa (Regulations can vary – check before you travel)	▲	▲	▲	▲	▲
Onward or Return Ticket	▲	▲	▲	▲	▲
Health Inoculations	▲	▲	▲	▲	▲
Health Documentation (➤ 9, Health Advice)	●	●	●	●	●
Travel Insurance	○	○	○	○	○
Driving Licence (national)	●	●	●	●	●
Car Insurance Certificate	●	●	●	●	●
Car Registration Document	●	●	●	●	●

ADVANCE PLANNING
WEBSITES
● Prague Information Service:
www.prague-info.cz
● City of Prague Official Guide:
www.welcometoPrague.cz

TOURIST INFORMATION
In the UK
Czech Tourism Great Britain
13 Harley Street, London
W1G 9QG
☎ (020) 7631 0427;
brochure line ☎ (090) 6364 0641
www.czechtourism.com

In the USA
Czech Tourism USA, 1109–1111
Madison Avenue, New York,
NY 10028 ☎ (212) 288 0830

In Canada
Czech Tourist Authority, 401 Bay
Street, Suite 1510 Simpson Tower,
Toronto, Ontario M5H 2Y4
☎ (416) 363 9928

In Australia
Czech Embassy, 8 Culgoa Circuit,
O'Malley, ACT 2606, Canberra
☎ (02) 6290 1386

HEALTH ADVICE
Medical insurance
All visitors to the Czech Republic
must carry health insurance to
cover any medical services whilst in
the country and/or hospital fees and
repatriation costs. EU Nationals
may be eligible for additional
medical care and should show their
passport when seeking medical
attention. US visitors should check
their insurance coverage.

Dental services
Dental treatment must be paid for.
Emergency 24-hour care is
available at Palackého 5, Nové
Město, Praha 1 ☎ 224 946 981.

TIME DIFFERENCES

GMT	Prague	Germany	USA (NY)	Netherlands	Spain
12 noon	1PM	1PM	7AM	1PM	1PM

The Czech Republic is on Central
European Time (GMT+1), but from
late March, when clocks are put
forward one hour, until late
October, Czech Summer Time
(GMT+2) operates.

WHAT'S ON WHEN

19 January *Jan Palach Day:* The country marks the day in 1969 when 20-year-old Charles University student Jan Palach died after setting fire to himself (on January 16) on Wenceslas Square to protest the invasion by Warsaw Pact troops the previous August,

and subsequent Soviet occupation of Czechoslovakia.

March *International Music Festival:* A series of classical and contemporary concerts is performed in venues all over the city throughout the month.

30 April *Witches' Night:* A bonfire held on Petřín Hill celebrates the traditional end of winter and the birth of spring.

Early May *Prague Spring:* A three-week event of classical music and dance, performed in churches, palaces and concert halls around Prague. The celebrations begin with a procession from Smetana's grave in Vyšehrad to his namesake concert hall in Obecní dům.

First week of June *Fringe Theatre Festival Prague:* This is a week of indoor and outdoor performances around the city by drama, music, comedy and dance troupes.

Late August *Festival of Italian Operas:* Puccini, Verdi and Rossini top the bill during this 10-day festival at the State Opera House.

Mid-September *Prague Autumn Music Festival:* Three weeks of classical music performances by orchestras and musicians from around the world.

Late September *Vinohrady Grape Harvest:* An annual celebration of the country's first grape harvest takes place in two main squares in the neighbourhood that was home to the Royal Vineyards during

NATIONAL HOLIDAYS

JAN	FEB	MAR	APR	MAY	JUN	JUL	AUG	SEP	OCT	NOV	DEC
1		(1)	(1)	2		2			1		3

1 Jan	New Year's Day	6 Jul	Jan Hus Day
Mar/Apr	Easter Monday	28 Sep	Czech Statehood Day
1 May	May Day	28 Oct	Independence Day
8 May	Liberation Day	17 Nov	Democracy Day
May/Jun	Whit Sunday and Monday	24–25 Dec	Christmas Eve/Day
5 Jul	St Cyril and St Method Day	26 Dec	St Stephen's Day

Restaurants, museums and other tourist attractions tend to stay open on these days.

Charles IV's reign. Traditional music and crafts along with plenty of *burčak* – the sweet but potent young wine.

Late October *International Jazz Festival:* For almost 30 years Prague has hosted this week-long festival of performances by jazz legends from the United States to Ukraine, with plenty of local stars in between.

17 November *Anniversary of the Velvet Revolution:* A commemoration and wreath-laying ceremony conducted on Wenceslas Square and Národní (although there has been much concern voiced by citizens recently about the poor attendance at this event).

December *Christmas market on Old Town Square:* Every festive season a giant Christmas tree lights up the centre of the square, while the space around it is crammed with market stalls selling carved toys, bobbin lace, ceramics, glass figurines, Christmas ornaments and tasty gingerbread cakes, barbecued sausages and *svarak* (mulled wine). Entertainment is provided by street performers.

Getting There

AIR

Prague's international airport is **Ruzyně Airport** (☎ 220 113 314) which has all the modern amenities you would expect of a European airport.

Czech Airlines – ČSA (☎ 239 007 007; **www.**csa.cz) operates direct scheduled flights to Prague from Britain, mainland Europe and North America. Flight time from London is 2 hours. Prague is connected by rail to all main European capitals (➤ 14, Getting Around). Other international carriers that fly into Prague include British Airways, Alitalia, KLM, Lufthansa, SAS and Air France.

Ruzyně Airport is 20km (12 miles) from the city centre and a 20- to 40-minute journey depending on your mode of transport.

Airport taxis are expensive, but AAA taxis are reasonably priced and have English-speaking operators (☎ 14014).

The next best method into town is on a **Cedaz minibus** (☎ 220 114 296) which run every 30 minutes between 5.30am and 9.30pm and will drop you at the Náměstí Republiky for around 90Kč per person. Cedaz will also take you or your whole party to your hotel for a reasonable set charge of a few hundred crowns. Look for the booth signed 'City Centre 90Kc'.

If you don't have a lot of luggage take the No 119 bus from the airport to Dejvická metro station. From there, take the main A-line into any of the four city-centre stations. This service runs every day from 5am–midnight, as do the buses.

RAIL

The overnight train from London – via Brussels and Cologne (information: ☎ 221 111 122; **www.**cdrail.cz) arrives at **Hlavní nádraží** which is on the 'C' (red) metro line. Inside the train station there is a tourist information office, ATM machines, exchange facilities and a 24-hour left-luggage office. It is a short walk from **Václavské náměstí** (Wenceslas Square). Some international trains also arrive at Prague's other main station **Nádraží Holešovice.** Several trams run along the park in front of the station.

BUS

International and national bus services arrive at **Florenc** bus and metro station on the east side of the city. The Old Town is then just a 5-minute walk or the B and C metro lines next door can take you anywhere else you want to go.

DRIVING

Driving is on the right.
Speed limit on motorways (annual toll payable):
130kph (80mph)
Minimum limit:
50kph (31mph)
Speed limit on country roads:
90kph (56mph) (on level crossings:
30kph/18mph)
Speed limit on urban roads:
50kph (31mph)
Seat belts must be worn in front seats – and rear seats where fitted. Under 12s may not travel in the front seat.

Drink driving *Don't* drink *any* alcohol if driving. The allowed blood/alcohol level is zero and penalties are severe.

Fuel Petrol *(benzín)* is sold in leaded form as *special* (91 octane) and *super* (96 octane). Unleaded petrol comes as *natural* (95 octane) and *super plus* (98 octane); the latter is available only at larger petrol stations. Diesel *(nafta)* is also available. In Prague, filling stations are few and far between, but some open 24 hours.

If you break down, ÚAMK, the Czech automobile club, operates a 24-hour nationwide breakdown service on the same terms as your own motoring club at home (non-members pay in full), ☎ 0123 (123 in Prague) or 154 from mobile phones. On motorways use emergency phones (every 2km/ 1 mile) to summon help.

Getting Around

TRANSPORTATION

Internal Flights Czech Airlines (ČSA ✉ V celnici 5, Praha 1 ☎ 239 007 007; **www**.csa.cz) and a variety of other carriers link Prague with Brno and Ostrava. Though not cheap, especially when compared with the train or bus, they are useful when you want to get somewhere quickly.

Trains Czech Railways (České Dráhy ☎ 221 111 122, 24-hours; **www**.cd.cz) run *rychlík* that stop only at major towns and *osobní* calling at every station. International trains to destinations outside the country leave from the main station Hlavní nádraží. Services to north and east Bohemia depart from Masarykovo nádraží; routes to the south are from Smíchovské nádraží.

River boats From April to September cruise boats ply the Vltava River, as far as Troja Château in the north of Prague and Slapy Lake in the south. The Prague Steamship Company (Pražská paroplavební společnost ☎ 2493 00 017; **www**.paroplavba.cz) is the main operator. There are usually boats tied up along the riverbank.

Metro Prague's metro is clean, fast and cheap. There are three lines: A (green), B (yellow) and C (red). Trains run 5am to midnight, every 2 minutes peak times (5 to 10 minutes other times). The letter 'M' with a downward arrow marks a station entrance. For information (also trams and buses) see **www**.dp-praha.cz/en/.

Trams/buses After the metro, trams *(tramvaj)* are the fastest way of getting around. There are 26 lines running every 6 to 8 minutes at peak times (10 to 15 minutes other times). Buses *(autobusy)* mainly keep out of the centre. There is one ticket for the metro, tram and bus. Tickets are available at *tabaks*, newspaper kiosks, metro stations and some tram stops (look for the yellow machine), and cost 14Kč single, 10Kč child. Multi-day passes are also available (3 days: 220Kč, 7 days: 280Kč, 15 days: 320Kč). Failure to produce a valid ticket on request will result in a 800Kč fine (400Kč on the spot).

DRIVING

A car is not necessary or advised in Prague as much of the city is off-limits to cars and parking is by permit only. If you're heading out of town, car rental is easy to arrange, but can be expensive. Shop around as some local firms charge less than well-known names. Try Dvořák Rent-a-Car (☎ 224 926 260) or Europcar (☎ 224 811 290).

TAXIS

Taxis abound in Prague. An unoccupied taxi has a lit-up sign and may be hailed on the street or hired from a taxi rank. Registered taxis should have a meter clearly displayed. Look for AAA, ProfiTaxi and City Taxi. You have the right to a printed receipt.

The Prague Card This three-day tourist pass provides entry to Prague Castle, all the city's major museums and historic buildings and for a bit more, unlimited travel on the metro, trams and bus. Adult card with transportation is 810Kč, or 590Kč without. Buy cards at Prague Information Service Offices at Staroměstská radnice, Hlavní nádraží station or Malostranská Mostecká vez (► 16). For further information, see **www.pis.cz/en.**

CONCESSIONS

Students/youths Holders of an International Student Identity Card (ISIC) are entitled to a 50 per cent reduction on admission to Prague's museums. Student cards also offer reductions on international trains, though not on domestic public transport. GTS (✉ Ve Smečkách 33, Praha 1 ☎ 222 211 204) specializes in travel for students and independent travellers.

Senior citizens There are no special senior citizen concessions. However, Saga Holidays organize holidays for over 50s and have trips to Prague (✉ Middelburg Square, Folkestone CT20 1AZ, UK ☎ 0800 414 383; **www.**saga.co.uk).

Being There

TOURIST OFFICES
Czech Tourist Authority
(Česká centrála cestovního ruchu)
✉ Vinohradská 46, 12041 Praha 2
☎ 221 580 111
www.czechtourism.com

Prague Information Service
(Pražská informační služba PIS)
✉ Staroměstská radnice (Old
Town Hall), Staroměstské náměstí,
Praha 1
☎ 224 482 202
www.prague-info.cz
🕐 Mon–Fri 8–7
Ⓜ Staroměstská

✉ Hlavní nádraží
(Main Railway Sation)
Wilsonova, Praha 1

🕐 Apr–Oct Mon–Fri 9–7, Sat–Sun
9–4; Nov–Mar Mon–Fri 9–6,
Sat–Sun 9–3
Ⓜ Hlavní nádraží

✉ Malostranská Mostecká vez,
(Lesser Town Tower), Mostecká,
Praha 1
🕐 Apr–Oct daily 10–6
Ⓜ Malostranská

Prague Tourist Centre
✉ Celetná 14, Karlova 1, Národní
4, Nerudova 4 (all Praha 1)
www.aroundprague.cz
🕐 Daily 9–8
Ⓜ Staroměstská

EMBASSIES AND CONSULATES
UK ☎ 257 402 111
Germany ☎ 257 531 481
USA ☎ 257 530 663
Netherlands ☎ 233 015 200
Spain ☎ 233 097 211

TELEPHONES
There are public telephones on the street and near metro stations. Local calls cost 4Kč and can only be made from

OPENING HOURS

- Shops
- Offices
- Banks
- Castles/châteaux
- Museums
- Pharmacies

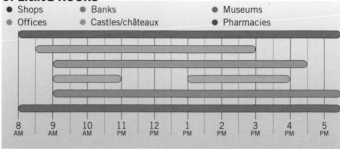

Some shops close for lunch but most open all day. On weekends, usual hours are Sat 10–7 and Sun 10–5. Grocery stores (*potraviny*) open from 7am; department stores and large shopping centres open until 8pm or 9pm. Outside Prague centre, shops are usually closed on Sunday except for malls in the suburbs. Some pharmacies open 24 hours. Banks vary, some open Saturday morning. Museums and art galleries usually open from 10–6; they are closed Mondays. Castles, châteaux and other historical monuments open daily (except Monday) May to September and weekends in April and October, but may be closed other times; please check.

the old orange phones which accept only 1Kč coins. Grey phones take 1, 2, 5 and 10Kč coins. There are also phonecard (*telefonní karta*) booths. Buy cards (200 and 300Kč) from post offices, *tabaks*, grocery stores and newsagents. Country code: 42, Prague city code: 02.

INTERNATIONAL DIALLING CODES

From Czech Republic to:
UK: 00 44
Germany: 00 49
USA: 00 1
Netherlands: 00 31
Spain: 00 34

EMERGENCY TELEPHONE NUMBERS

Police:
☎ 112 or 158
Ambulance:
☎ 112 or 155
Fire:
☎ 112 or 150

POSTAL SERVICES
Post offices

Post offices have distinctive orange *Pošta* signs. The main post office (✉ Jindřišská 14, Nové Město, Praha 1) is open daily 24 hours. There are several branches in the city which are open 8am–7pm (noon Sat) and closed Sun (☎ 221 131 445, non-English speaker).

ELECTRICITY

The power supply in the Czech Republic is 220 volts. Plugs are of the two-round-pin variety, so an adaptor is needed for most non-Continental European appliances and a voltage transformer for appliances operating on 100–120 volts.

CURRENCY AND FOREIGN EXCHANGE

The monetary unit of the Czech Republic is the Koruna česká (Kč) – or Czech crown – which is divided into 100 haléř – or heller. There are coins of 10, 20 and 50 hellers and 1, 2, 5, 10, 20 and 50 crowns. Banknotes come in 20, 50, 100, 200, 500, 1,000 and 5,000 crowns. Money may be changed at the airport, in banks (▶ 17, Opening Hours), major hotels, Čedok offices, and in the centre of Prague at exchange offices. Exchange offices advertising 'No Commission' are usually a poor place to change money and the no commission policy only applies if you're changing large amounts of money.

TIPS/GRATUITIES

Yes ✓ No ✗		
Hotels	✗	
Restaurants	✓	10%
Cafés/bars	✓	10%
Taxis	✓	10%
Tour guides	✓	20Kč
Porters	✓	40Kč
Hairdressers	✓	10%
Cloakroom attendants	✓	2Kč
Theatre/cinema usherettes	✗	
Toilets	✓	2Kč

HEALTH AND SAFETY

Sun advice The sun is not a real problem in Prague. June to August is the sunniest (and hottest) period but there are often thunder showers to cool things down. If the summer sun is fierce, apply a sunscreen and wear a hat, or visit a museum.

Drugs Pharmacies (*lékárna* or *apothéka*) are the only places to sell over-the-counter medicines. They also dispense many drugs (*leky*) normally available only by prescription in other Western countries.

Safe water Tap water is perfectly safe but heavily chlorinated so it can have a metallic taste. Bottled water is available everywhere: *né perlivá* is still water, *jemně perlivá* is lightly carbonated and *perlivá* is carbonated.

Personal safety Prague is a comparatively safe city, though petty crime is on the increase in central areas. Report any loss or theft to the *městská policie* (municipal police) – black uniforms.
● Watch your bag in tourist areas, and on the metro/trams, especially trams 22 and 23.
● Deposit your passport and valuables in the hotel safe.
● Never leave valuables in your car.

CLOTHING SIZES

Czech Republic	UK	Rest of Europe	USA	
46	36	46	36	
48	38	48	38	
50	40	50	40	
52	42	52	42	
54	44	54	44	**Suits**
56	46	56	46	
41	7	41	8	
42	7.5	42	8.5	
43	8.5	43	9.5	
44	9.5	44	10.5	
45	10.5	45	11.5	**Shoes**
46	11	46	12	
37	14.5	37	14.5	
38	15	38	15	
39/40	15.5	39/40	15.5	
41	16	41	16	
42	16.5	42	16.5	**Shirts**
43	17	43	17	
34	8	34	6	
36	10	36	8	
38	12	38	10	
40	14	40	12	
42	16	42	14	**Dresses**
44	18	44	16	
38	4.5	38	6	
38	5	38	6.5	
39	5.5	39	7	
39	6	39	7.5	
40	6.5	40	8	**Shoes**
41	7	41	8.5	

Best places to see

1

Chrám svatého Mikuláš (St Nicholas's Church)

www.psalterium.cz

The all-powerful Jesuit Order commissioned this superb church, the ultimate expression of Prague baroque, at the beginning of the 18th century.

Restored at a cost of 120 million Czech crowns, this monumental building was constructed between 1704 and 1756 by father-and-son team,

Christoph and Kilián Dientzenhofer, and completed by Kilián's son-in-law, Anselmo Lurago. The interior decoration builds on an accumulation of *trompe l'oeil* effects, culminating in *The Apotheosis of St Nicholas* by Johann Kracker, a fresco covering more than 1,500sq m (1,795sq yds) of the nave ceiling. The splendid dome is 18m (59ft) higher than the Petřín Tower. But not everything is as costly as it appears. Many of the mottled pink and green pillars and other details are *faux marbre*, while the four more than life-size statues under the dome are made of wood, with a surface covering of glazed chalk. These dramatic characterizations of the Church Fathers include a vigorous St Cyril triumphantly lancing the devil with his crozier. The sculptor, Ignaz Platzer, also created the copper statue of St Nicholas, which looks down from the high altar. Also of note is the rococo pulpit, overhanging with angels and cherubs, which was made by Peter and Richard Práchner in 1765. The baroque organ, played by Mozart in 1787, boasts 2,500 pipes and 44 registers. Four years later it was played at a funeral Mass in his memory. The church was full to overflowing, evidence of the esteem in which he was held here.

✠ 133 C5 ✉ Malostranské náměstí, Malá Strana, Praha 1 🕐 Mar–Oct daily 9–5; Nov–Feb daily 9–4. Concerts Wed–Mon at 6pm ✋ Inexpensive 🍴 Cafés (£), restaurants (££–£££) near by 🚇 Malostranská 🚊 12, 20, 22, 23

2 Josefov

www.jewishmuseum.cz

For more than 700 years this attractive neighbourhood of the Old Town has been home to Prague's Jewish community.

Jewish people first settled in the Old Town in the 12th century. In 1254 the area was surrounded by a ghetto wall, following a decree of the third Lateran Council. The ghetto was a centre of learning, with its own Talmudic school and Hebrew printing press. Although Prague's Jews were regularly subjected to discrimination and persecution, wealthy elders, like Mayor Mordechai Maisel in the 16th century, won privileges for the ghetto by placing their wealth at the disposal of the imperial treasury. In 1784 Emperor Joseph II relaxed many restrictions, and in 1849 Josefov (as the Jewish quarter was now called) was incorporated into the city. Most of the ghetto slums were demolished at the end of the 19th century. The Holocaust all but wiped out the Jewish population of Prague – today's community numbers only about 1,000.

Hitler planned a museum in Josefov recording the history of the 'extinct' Jewish race. Ironically, this ensured the preservation of treasures and furnishings confiscated from synagogues all over

Bohemia and Moravia. They are now exhibited in three of the restored synagogues. The Pinkas Synagogue is a particularly poignant Holocaust memorial. Also in Josefov are the Old Jewish Cemetery and the oldest synagogue in Europe: the Old-New Synagogue, which has been the focus of religious worship since the 13th century. The Jewish Town Hall, dating from 1763, is a baroque building with a distinctive green steeple. Set in one of the gables is a clock with hands that travel anti-clockwise, following the Hebrew lettering, read from the right.

✚ 134 C3 ✉ U Staré Školy 1, Josefov, Praha 1 ☎ 222 317 191 🕐 Apr–Oct Sun–Fri 9–6; Nov–Mar Sun–Fri 9–4.30. Closed Jewish hols 👛 Moderate. Jewish Museum ticket includes most synagogues, the cemetery and Ceremonial Hall
🚇 Staroměstská 🚌 17, 18

3 Katedrála svatého Víta (St Vitus's Cathedral)

www.hrad.cz

St Vitus's took nearly six centuries to complete and was consecrated only in 1929, yet it stands on the site of a chapel founded in 925.

Work started on the present Gothic building in 1344, under the direction of Matthias of Arras. German Petr Parléř and his two sons were responsible for the lofty choir and the surrounding chapels, which were finally completed early in the 15th century. The tower on the south side was given its Renaissance steeple in 1562, to which baroque embellishments were later added. The nave and the impressive west end date from the second half of the 19th century. The Golden Portal (the original entrance) on the south side contains a mosaic of the Last Judgement, dating from 1370, which has been restored to its former glory.

The Chapel of St Wenceslas, dating from 1358 to 1367, is one of the oldest parts of the building and the most beautifully decorated. The lower walls are encrusted with scintillating jasper and amethyst, while the frescoes (14th–16th centuries) depict scenes from the passion of Christ and the life of St Wenceslas (the saint is buried directly underneath the chapel). The foundations of the 11th-century Romanesque basilica were unearthed as the cathedral was nearing completion and can be seen in the crypt, along with the sarcophagi of the kings of Bohemia. King Vladislav Jagiello

commissioned the beautiful Royal Oratory in the 1480s: the vaulted ceiling, shaped like the branches of a tree, is highly unusual. An exquisite silver funerary monument to the cult saint, John of Nepomuk, was erected in the choir in 1736. One of the cherubs points to the saint's tongue, which was said never to have decayed. The cathedral also contains fine 20th-century stained glass, notably Alphonse Mucha's portrait of saints Cyril and Methodius in the third chapel from the west end.

✠ 132 B4 ✉ Pražský hrad, Hradčany, Praha 1 ☎ None
🕐 Apr–Oct daily 9–5; Nov–Mar daily 9–4 💷 Free;
moderate charge for crypt, tower and choir 🍴 Café (£),
restaurants (££–£££) near by Ⓜ Malostranská 🚋 22, 23
to Pražský hrad

4 Loreta

www.loreta.cz

This pretty baroque shrine has been a place of pilgrimage since 1626, when it was endowed by a Bohemian noblewoman, Kateřina of Lobkowicz.

The Loreta shrine was inspired by a medieval legend. In 1278, so the story goes, the Virgin Mary's house in Nazareth was miraculously transported by angels to Loreto in Italy and thus saved from the Infidel. The Marian cult became an important propaganda weapon of the Counter-Reformation and, following the defeat of the Protestants at the Battle of the White Mountain in 1620, some 50 other Loreto shrines were founded in Bohemia and Moravia.

The heart of the Loreta is the Santa Casa, a replica of the Virgin's relocated house. Sumptuously decorated, it incorporates a beam and several bricks from the Italian original. On the

silver altar (behind a grille) is a small ebony statue of the Virgin. The rich stucco reliefs, depicting scenes from the lives of the prophets, are by Italian artists.

The much larger Church of the Nativity was designed by Kilián Dientzenhofer between 1734 and 1735, with ceiling frescoes by Václav Reiner and Johann Schöpf. Less edifying are the gruesome remains of saints Felecissimus and Marcia, complete with wax death masks. The cloisters, originally 17th century but with an upper storey added by Dientzenhofer in the 1740s, once provided overnight shelter for pilgrims. In the corner chapel of Our Lady of Sorrows is a diverting painting of St Starosta, a bearded lady who prayed for facial hair to put off an unwanted suitor, only to be crucified by her father whose plans for her wedding were thwarted. The Loreta treasury has a famed collection of vestments and other religious objects, including a diamond monstrance made in Vienna in 1699, which glitters with 6,200 precious stones.

🕂 132 C2 ✉ Loretánské náměstí 7, Hradčany, Praha 1 ☎ 220 516 740 🕐 Tue–Sun 9–12.15, 1–4.30 🖐 Inexpensive 🚌 22, 23

5 Pražský hrad (Prague Castle)

www.hrad.cz

Dominating Hradčany with majestic assurance, Prague Castle has a history stretching back more than a thousand years and is still the Czech State's administrative centre.

The Castle's château-like appearance dates from 1753 to 1775, when the Empress of Austria, Maria-Theresa, ordered its reconstruction, but the Gothic towers and spires of St Vitus's Cathedral are clues to a much older history. Many misfortunes took their toll on the churches and palaces, culminating in a disastrous fire in 1541 which engulfed the whole of Hradčany. Architecturally this was a blessing in disguise and the extensive restoration work resulted in the stunning Renaissance and baroque interiors of today's Royal Palace.

Entry to the Castle is through a series of enclosed courtyards. In the first, the changing of the guard takes place hourly in the shadow of huge baroque sculptures of battling Titans. The entrance to the second courtyard is through the Matthias Gate, which dates from 1614. Directly opposite is the 19th-century Chapel of the Cross, now the Information Centre. On the other side of the courtyard, the Picture Gallery of Prague Castle contains paintings from the Imperial collections, including minor works by Titian, Tintoretto, Veronese and Rubens. The third courtyard is dominated by St Vitus's Cathedral (➤ 26–27). To

the right, the 18th-century façade of the Royal Palace conceals a network of halls and chambers on various levels, dating from the Romanesque period onwards. The centrepiece is the magnificent Vladislav Hall. To the right are the former offices of the Chancellery of Bohemia, dating from the early 16th century, where, on 23 May 1618, after learning of the accession to the throne of the detested Archduke Ferdinand of Habsburg, more than 100 Protestant noblemen burst into the far room and threw two Catholic governors and a secretary out of the window. The officials survived the fall but the incident, known as the Defenestration of Prague, marked the start of the Thirty Years' War. The Diet Hall next door was designed by the Renaissance architect Bonifaz Wohlmut in 1563 and its walls are hung with portraits of the Habsburgs. The Riders' Staircase leads down to the remains of the Romanesque and Gothic Palaces and an exhibition on the castle.

The Castle complex's other outstanding monument is St George's Basilica (➤ 67) and a short walk away is the Lobkowicz Palace. Beyond Golden Lane, the Daliborka Tower is named after a nobleman imprisoned here on suspicion of complicity in a peasants' revolt. In the Mihulka, or Powder Tower, alchemists were once employed to elicit the secret of turning base metals into gold.

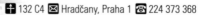

✚ 132 C4 ✉ Hradčany, Praha 1 ☎ 224 373 368
🕐 Apr–Oct daily 9–5; Nov–Mar daily 9–4 ✋ Moderate
🍴 Cafés (£), restaurants (££–£££) 🚊 22, 23 ❓ Changing of the guard every hour on the hour at the main gate. Information centre in the third courtyard.

6 Staroměstská radnice (Old Town Hall)

www.pis.cz

The star attraction of Prague's most famous landmark is the enchanting Astronomical Clock.

The Old Town Hall is actually a row of houses adapted over the centuries by the council. In 1338 the burghers enlarged the merchant Volflin's house, and the tower and chapel were added in 1381. Neighbouring Křiž House was acquired in 1387. The house of furrier Mikš was added in 1548 and the house At the Cock in the 19th century.

The main attraction is the Astronomical Clock, which gives the time of day, the months and seasons of the year, the signs of the zodiac, the course of the sun and the holidays of the Christian calendar. On the hour, the figure of Death rings a bell and the 12 Apostles appear above. A cock crows and time is up for the Turk, who shakes his head in disbelief; the Miser, who eyes his bag of gold; and Vanity, who admires himself in a mirror.

Inside are the council chamber where Bohemian kings were elected, and a chapel with a distinctive oriel window. Climb the clock tower for views across the red rooftops of the city.

➕ 134 D4 ✉ Staroměstské náměstí 1, Staré Město, Praha 1 ☎ 236 002 562 🕐 8 Feb–Oct Mon 11–6, Tue–Sun 9–6; Nov–7 Feb Mon 11–5, Tue–Sun 9–5 💷 Moderate 🍴 Cafés (££), restaurants (£££) near by 🚇 Staroměstská 🚊 17, 18 ❓ Tourist information office open all year.

7

Šternberský palác (Sternberg Palace)

www.ngprague.cz

The 17th-century baroque palace, built for Count Wenceslas Sternberg from 1698 to 1707, now houses the National Gallery's impressive collection of Old Masters.

The palace is set back from Hradčany Square (► 65): access is through the left-hand entrance of the Archbishop's Palace. The exhibition is arranged

chronologically by the artists' country of origin. The gallery's proudest possession is Albrecht Dürer's *Feast of the Rose Garlands* (1506), acquired by Emperor Rudolph II because it features one of his ancestors, Maximilian I (shown in the foreground with Pope Julius II). German painting is also represented by Holbein the Elder and Lucas Cranach, including a charming *Adam and Eve*. There are works by Geertgen tot Sint Jans, Jan Gossaert and the Brueghels, father and son. Pieter Brueghel the Elder's animated calendar painting, *The Haymaking* has a rhythmic, almost dance-like quality. Outstanding among the later work is a portrait by Rembrandt, *Scholar in his Study* (1634), and several paintings by Rubens, including *Martyrdom of St Thomas* (1637–39), which was commissioned for the church in Malá Strana. By comparison, the Italian Renaissance is less well represented, although Andrea della Robbia, Sebastiano del Piombo and Pietro della Francesca all feature in the collection and there are some fine altar panels by the 14th-century Sienese artist, Pietro Lorenzetti. Paintings by artists of the 18th-century Venetian school, including Tiepolo and Canaletto, and two fine Spanish works, El Greco's *Head of Christ* and a portrait by Goya of Don Miguel de Lardizabal, can also be found in the gallery. The superb collection of 19th- and 20th-century French art is now in the Veletrzny Palace (➤ 40–41).

🚩 132 B3 ✉ Hradčanské náměstí 15, Hradčany, Praha 1
☎ 220 514 634 🕐 Tue–Sun 10–6 ✋ Inexpenive; free first Wed of the month 🍴 Café (££) 🚇 Malostranská 🚌 22, 23 to Pražský hrad

8 Strahovský klášter (Strahov Monastery)

www.strahovskyklaster.cz

Strahovní means 'watching over', and this ancient religious foundation, famous as a centre of learning, has been guarding the western approaches to Hradčany since the 12th century.

Above the baroque gateway is a statue of the founder of the Premonstratensian Order, St Norbert; to the left of the gate is the Church of St Roch, patron saint of plague victims, commissioned by Rudolf II in 1603 after Prague had narrowly escaped an epidemic. It is now used for modern art exhibitions. The twin-towered Abbey Church of the Nativity has a Romanesque core, but its present appearance dates from around 1750, when Anselmo Lurago remodelled the western façade. Mozart played the organ here on two occasions. The vaulted ceiling is sumptuously decorated with cartouches and frescoes by Jiří Neunhertz, depicting the legend of St Norbert, whose remains were brought here from Magdeburg in 1627 and reburied in the chapel of St Ursula, on the left of the nave.

The library of the Strahov Monastery is more than 800 years old and among the

finest in Europe. The Theological Hall, built between 1671 and 1679 by Giovanni Orsi, has walls lined with elaborately carved bookcases, stacked with precious volumes and manuscripts. The Philosophical Hall dates from 1782 to 1784, and its entire ceiling is covered with a delightful composition entitled *The Spiritual Development of Mankind*, by Franz Maulbertsch. The library contains over 130,000 volumes, including 2,500 books published before 1500, and 3,000 manuscripts. The oldest book, the 9th-century *Strahov Gospels*, is on show in the entrance.

✠ 132 D3 ✉ Strahovské nádvoří 1/132, Hradčany, Praha 1
☎ 233 107 718 🕐 Library: daily 9–noon, 1–5; Gallery: 9–noon, 12.30–5. Closed Christmas and Easter
✋ Moderate 🍴 Restaurant (££) 🚌 22, 23 to Pohořelec

9 Václavské náměstí (Wenceslas Square)

Wenceslas Square really comes alive after dark, when its restaurants, cinemas and nightclubs attract a boisterous crowd.

Prague's most famous thoroughfare is actually an impressive 750m-long (898yd) boulevard, dominated at the northern end by Josef Schulz's neo-Renaissance National Museum (➤ 102). Once staging a horse market, Wenceslas Square was

later a focus for political demonstration. When the Soviet army occupied Prague in August 1968 it was here that the distraught population gathered to protest. Several months later a student, Jan Palach, burned himself to death on the steps of the National Museum. Following the collapse of the Communist regime in December 1989, Václav Havel and Alexander Dubcek appeared on the balcony of No 36 to greet their ecstatic supporters. Palach and other victims of the regime are commemorated in a small shrine in front of Josef Myslbek's equestrian statue of St Wenceslas.

Wenceslas Square became a showcase for modern Czech architecture when the traditional two- and three-storey baroque houses were demolished in the 19th century. The neo-Renaissance Wiehl House was completed in 1896 and is decorated with florid sgraffito and statuary by Mikuláš Aleš. Many of the sumptuous art nouveau interiors and fittings in the Europa Hotel (No 25) have survived and are also worth investigating. The functionalist Koruna palác (No 1), a covered shopping arcade with a stunning glass dome dating from 1911, became the model for other passageways linking the square with the neighbouring streets (the Lucerna, at No 61, was built by Václav Havel's grandfather). The former insurance offices on the corner of Jindřišská could well have been the stuff of nightmares for Franz Kafka when he worked here as a clerk from 1906 to 1907.

➕ 135 E5 ✉ Václavské náměstí, Nové Město, Praha 1 🎟 Free 🚇 Můstek, Muzeum 🚋 3, 9, 14

10 Veletržní palác (Veletrzny Palace)

www.ngprague.cz

The gallery's outstanding collection of modern Czech and European art is housed in a 1920s constructivist palace.

Designed by Oldřich Tyl and Josef Fuchs for the Prague Trade Fair of 1928, the enormous glass-fronted building was described by the famous modernist architect, Le Corbusier, as 'breathtaking'. The priceless French collection runs the gamut of Impressionist and post-Impressionist artists. Among the highlights are *Two Women among the Flowers* by Monet (1875), *Green Rye* by Van Gogh (1889), and one of Gauguin's Tahiti paintings, *Flight*

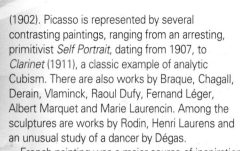

(1902). Picasso is represented by several contrasting paintings, ranging from an arresting, primitivist *Self Portrait*, dating from 1907, to *Clarinet* (1911), a classic example of analytic Cubism. There are also works by Braque, Chagall, Derain, Vlaminck, Raoul Dufy, Fernand Léger, Albert Marquet and Marie Laurencin. Among the sculptures are works by Rodin, Henri Laurens and an unusual study of a dancer by Dégas.

French painting was a major source of inspiration for Czech artists seeking an alternative to the predominant German culture of the late 19th century. Jan Zrzavy, Bohumil Kubišta and Emil Filla all progressed from neo-Impressionism to more abstract styles. Kubišta's *Still Life with Funnel* (1910) was directly influenced by a similar study by Picasso. Other artists producing Cubist works at the time include Filla, Václav Špála and the sculptor Otto Gutfreund. The Czechs' affinity with French art becomes even more noticeable in the inter-war period, when the two countries were closely bound together by political and diplomatic ties. The crowning moment came in 1935, when the founder of the Surrealist movement, André Breton, visited Czechoslovakia at the invitation of the Prague Surrealists, Jindřich Štyrský, Vincenc Makovsky and Toyen (Marie Čermínová). The exhibition concludes with sections on post-war and contemporary art.

✚ 140 E4 ✉ Dukelských hrdinů 47, Holešovice, Praha 7
☎ 224 301 024 🕐 Tue–Sun 10–6 👐 Moderate
🍴 Restaurant (££); internet café (£) Ⓜ Vltavská 🚌 5, 12, 17 to Veletržni 🚆 Holešovice

Exploring

The view from the Charles Bridge at dusk: in the foreground, a procession of dramatic sculptures recedes into the distance; assembled behind them an extraordinary composition of gilded crosses, tented Gothic towers and baroque domes is silhouetted against the sunset. This is Prague in a nutshell. The city's extraordinary charms lie in the painstaking detail of its architecture – a gabled roof, an ornate railing, a sculpted house sign, a pair of Atlantes supporting a portal, a votive statue ensconced in a niche, a street lamp decorated with dancing maidens. Wherever you turn there is some magic to catch the eye.

This book focuses on Central Prague (Praha 1) which is divided into the following districts: Staré Město (Old Town), Nové Město (New Town), Malá Strana (Lesser Quarter), Josefov (Jewish Quarter) and Hradčany (Castle Quarter). Where reference has been made to anything in the outlying areas (Praha 2–10), the district name and Prague area number are given, eg Holešovice, Praha 7.

Staré Město Area

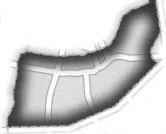

Beyond the Charles Bridge is Staré Město (Old Town), historically the most important of the areas that make up this great city. Staré Město is positioned on a bend in the Vltava River and grew up around Staroměstské náměstí (Old Town Square), still a popular meeting place and one of the prettiest squares in Europe, then stretching down to Karlův most (Charles Bridge) and east out to Celetná.

The southern section of Staré Město is a maze of narrow streets and arcaded courtyards that conceal gabled houses, brightly painted shop-fronts, churches and taverns. The streets are so narrow that trams have to make their way around the Old Town and not through it as kings once did en route to their coronations, when Staré Město was part of the 'Royal Route'. Contrasts abound here with steep Gothic spires and colourful baroque palaces standing alongside junk shops and internet cafés and fine restaurants next to more earthy pubs.

BETLÉMSKÁ KAPLE (BETHLEHEM CHAPEL)

The Bethlehem Chapel was built by followers of the radical
preacher Jan Milíč of Kroměříž between 1391 and 1394. In 1402
Jan Hus, was appointed rector and drew huge crowds to his
sermons, which were given in Czech, rather than Latin. Hus was a
charismatic figure, but his attacks on the wealth and corruption of
the Catholic hierarchy did not endear him to his religious superiors.

He eventually overstepped the bounds of orthodoxy, arguing that the Pope had no authority over the Bohemian Church and that doctrine should be based on the scriptures alone. Hus was excommunicated in 1412 and the Bethlehem Chapel was closed. Summoned to defend his teachings at the Council of Constance two years later, Hus consented to leave the safe territory of Prague only after being issued with a guarantee of safe conduct by the Emperor Sigismund. But the Emperor went back on his word: Hus was arrested, condemned as a heretic and, on 6 July 1415, burned at the stake.

The decision to reconstruct the Chapel was taken in 1949. The prayer hall is trapezoid in form, the timber roof resting on plain stone supports. The total area measures 798sq m (8,590sq ft) – ample space for the congregations of 3,000 who came to hear Hus speak. Upstairs in the former preacher's house is an exhibition: 'The Bethlehem Chapel in Czech history and the tradition of non-Catholic thinking'.

✚ 134 D3 ✉ Betlémské náměstí 4, Staré Město ☎ 224 248 595 🕐 Apr–Oct daily 10–6.30; Nov–Mar Tue–Sun 10–5.30. Closed 1 Jan, Easter Mon, 1 and 8 May, 5–6 July, 28 Oct, 24–26 Dec ✋ Moderate 🍴 Cafés (£) near by 🚇 Národní třída 🚌 6, 9, 18, 22

CELETNÁ

The street of bakers is one of the oldest in the city and was on the royal processional route. Its handsomely decorated baroque façades conceal in many cases Romanesque or Gothic foundations. An exception is the Cubist House of the Black Madonna (➤ 48). The house at No 36 is the former mint. Some of Prague's best known restaurants are on Celetná: House At the Golden Vulture (No 22), At the Spider (No 17) and At the Golden Stag (No 11). Celetná is also a good place to shop for glassware, jewellery and antiques.

✚ 135 D5 ✉ Celetná, Staré Město ✋ Free 🍴 Cafés (££), restaurants (£££) 🚇 Náměstí Republiky

DŮM PÁNŮ Z KUNŠTÁTU A PODĚBRAD (HOUSE OF THE LORDS OF KUNSTAT AND PODEBRAD)

The medieval chambers of this former palace, with original Romanesque cross-vaulted ceilings and fireplaces, are now open to the public. Dating from about 1200, they once formed the ground floor of a building which was enlarged in the 15th century for the Lords of Kunstat and Podebrad. There is a small exhibition on its most famous resident, George of Podebrad, who became King of Bohemia in 1457.

➕ 134 D3 ✉ Řetězová 3, Staré Město ☎ 224 212 299 🕒 May–Sep Tue–Sun 10–6 Ⓜ Národní třída 🖐 Moderate 🚌 6, 9, 18, 22, 23

DŮM U ČERNÉ MATKY BOŽÍ (HOUSE OF THE BLACK MADONNA)

While Cubist painting is common in Europe, Cubist architecture is unique to Bohemia. Designed by Josef Gočár between 1911 and 1912, this innovative building was right at the cutting edge of the modernist movement, with its façades broken into multiple planes in order to create an unusual interplay of light and shade. Behind a grille on the first floor is the statue of the Madonna which gives the building its name. Upstairs is a beautiful café that looks just as it did when it opened in the 1920s.

Inside is a permanent exhibition on Czech Cubism from 1911 to 1919.

➕ 135 D5 ✉ Ovocný trh 19, Staré Město ☎ 224 211 746 🕒 Tue–Sun 10–6. Closed 1 Jan, Easter Mon, 1 and 8 May, 5 and 6 July, 28 Oct, 24–6 Dec 🖐 Moderate Ⓜ Náměstí Republiky 🚌 5, 8, 14

DŮM U KAMENNÉHO ZVONU
(HOUSE AT THE STONE BELL)

This magnificent Gothic tower with its characteristic hipped roof
was built as a palace for King John of Luxembourg around 1340.
The sculpted decoration of the west façade was rediscovered in
the 1960s, having long been concealed by a rococo face-lift.
Make sure you don't overlook the stone bell on the corner of the
building which gives the house its name. Concerts and exhibitions
are held here and visitors can see original Gothic features,
including extensive fragments of medieval wall painting. The
ceiling beams, delicately painted with floral motifs, date from the
reign of Charles IV.

✚ 134 C4 ✉ Staroměstské náměstí 13, Staré Město ☎ 224 827 526
🕐 Tue–Sun 10–6. Closed 1 Jan, Easter Mon, 1 and 8 May, 5–6 Jul, 28 Oct,
24–6 Dec ✋ Inexpensive 🚇 Staroměstská

KARLŮV MOST (CHARLES BRIDGE)

This remarkable sandstone bridge, designed in 1357 by Petr Parléř for King Charles IV, links the Old Town with the Lesser Quarter. In 1657 a bronze crucifix with a Hebrew inscription was erected on the bridge – the only ornament at that time. The idea caught on and now more than 30 sculptures adorn the parapets. Perhaps the finest of them, by Matthias Braun (1710), shows St Luitgard kissing Christ's wounds in a vision. The figure with the starry halo is St John of Nepomuk whose tortured body was hurled into the river from this spot in 1393 after he had dared to side with his archbishop against the king. The Old Town Bridge Tower, built in 1391, is also the work of Parléř. The sculptures above the arch show St Vitus in the company of kings Wenceslas IV and Charles IV. Today, buskers and street traders bring the bridge to life.

✚ 134 D2 ✉ Karlův most, Staré Město ⊙ Malá Strana Tower: Apr–Oct daily 10–6. Staré Město Tower: Apr–May, Oct daily 10–7; Jun–Sep daily 10–10; Mar daily 10–6; Nov–Feb daily 10–5 ✋ Towers: inexpensive ⊙ Staroměstská 🚌 12, 22

KAROLINUM

Founded in 1348 by Charles IV, the Karolinum is the oldest university in Central Europe. It acquired the house of the former mint master, Johlin Rothlev, in 1383 (until then classes had been held in churches or private houses). Although Rothlev's house was remodelled in the 18th century by František Kaňka, the exquisite oriel window protruding from the façade on Ovocný trh is a reminder of its medieval origins. The Karolinum's original premises are currently occupied by the university Rectorate.

✚ 134 D4 ✉ Železná 9, Staré Město ☎ 224 491 250; www.cuni.cz ⊙ Můstek

KLEMENTINUM

When the Emperor Ferdinand I invited the Jesuits to Prague in 1556 to spearhead the Counter-Reformation, they moved into the former monastery of St Clement. In the 17th century the Karolinum (➤ 51) merged with the Klementinum and they undertook a building programme which lasted over 150 years.

The walls of the baroque fortress enclosed a college, schools, churches, a library, a theatre, an observatory and a printing shop. When the Jesuit Order was dissolved in 1773 the complex was taken over by the university; today it belongs to the National Library. The Chapel of Mirrors (1724–30) is also open for concerts.

✚ 134 D3 ✉ Klementinum 190, Staré Město ☎ 221 663 111 ◷ May–Oct Mon–Fri 2–7, Sat–Sun 10–7; Mar–Apr, Nov–Dec Mon–Fri 2–6, Sat–Sun 11–7 ✋ Moderate Ⓜ Staroměstská 🚌 17, 18

KOSTEL PANNY MARIE PŘED TÝNEM (CHURCH OF OUR LADY BEFORE TÝN)

Most impressive at night when its gaunt, black steeples are eerily lit, Our Lady before Týn is the Old Town parish church. Although building started in 1380 under the supervision of Petr Parléř, work on the towers was not completed until 1511. For most of that period Týn Church was the stronghold of the Hussite Utraquists, who insisted on taking communion wine as well as bread (the symbolic gilded chalice which hung from the gable was melted down after the Counter-Reformation to make an effigy of the Virgin). The sculpted portal dates from 1390. The interior is a mix of Gothic and baroque styles. Over the high altar are paintings by Karel Škréta, dating from 1640 to 1660, while Gothic features include a pietà and a pewter font (1414). In front of the high altar is the tomb of the Danish astronomer, Tycho Brahe (1546–1601).

✚ 134 C4 ✉ Staroměstské náměstí, Staré Město ☎ 222 322 801 ◷ Services Wed–Sat at 6pm, Sun 9.30am and 9pm ✋ Free 🍴 Cafés (£), restaurants (£££) near by Ⓜ Staroměstská

KOSTEL SVATÉHO JAKUBA
(ST JAMES'S CHURCH)

The Minorite Order of Franciscans commissioned this baroque church in 1689 after its 13th-century predecessor had been destroyed in a fire. The paintings in the nave, galleries and 21 side altars are by a variety of artists, including Franz Voget, Peter Brandl and Václav Reiner, who also contributed the effulgent *Martyrdom of St James* over the high altar. Equally remarkable is the stunning tomb of the Chancellor of Bohemia, Count Vratislav of Mitrovice, on the left-hand side of the nave. It was sculpted in marble and sandstone by Ferdinand Brokoff. A shrivelled arm which dangles just inside the door belonged to a jewel thief caught stealing here in the 16th century.

St James's is renowned for its musical tradition. A choir sings at high Mass on Sundays, accompanied on a splendid baroque organ dating from 1702. There are regular concerts and recitals here.

✠ 135 C5 ✉ Malá Štupartská 6, Staré Město 🕐 Mon–Sat 9.30–12.15, 2–4. Sun except for services 8, 9, 10.30, also for concerts ♿ Free 🚇 Můstek

KŘIŽOVNICKÉ NÁMĚSTÍ
(KNIGHTS OF THE CROSS SQUARE)

Dominating the eastern side of this square, which is named after the 13th-century guardians of the Judith Bridge and which is a popular place, is the façade of the Klementinum and the Jesuit Church of St Saviour (➤ 53). The knights' own Church of St Francis, a baroque building which dates from 1679 to 1688, is across the square. The church's dome is thought

to have been modelled on the dome of St Peter's in Rome.

An exhibition at the side of the church includes a visit to the medieval crypt, which is decorated with garishly painted baroque stalactites. The treasury contains a collection of jewelled monstrances, chalices, reliquaries and other religious objects which belonged to the Order, some dating back to the 16th century. Perhaps of greatest interest is a surviving span of the 12th-century Judith Bridge, complete with water stairs.

Standing in front of the church, near today's Charles Bridge, is an imposing statue of Charles IV, designed in 1848 by Jan Bendl.

✠ 134 D2 ✉ Křižovnické náměstí, Staré Město ⓘ Exhibition: Apr–Oct Tue–Sun 10–6; Nov–Mar Tue–Sun 10–5 💰 Inexpensive ⓜ Staroměstská 🚊 17, 18

MUZEUM BEDŘICHA SMETANY (SMETANA MUSEUM)

The life and work of the 'father of Czech Music', Bedřich Smetana (1824–84), are traced here through letters, documents, scores and musical instruments. Smetana studied piano and composition in Prague, where he heard Liszt and, later, Berlioz perform. A fervent patriot, whose music helped inspire the Czech national revival of the 19th century, he is best known abroad for his emotionally charged symphonic

poem, *Ma vlast* (My homeland) – the famous second movement evokes the swirling currents of the Vltava. He also composed some fine chamber music, as well as numerous operas for the National Theatre, including *The Bartered Bride* and *The Kiss*. Smetana's later life was clouded by personal tragedy: in 1874 he went profoundly deaf after suffering from tinnitus and later lost his reason, dying in an asylum.

🕂 134 D2 ✉ Novotného lávka 1, Staré Město ☎ 222 222 082 🕔 Wed–Mon 10–12, 12.30–5 ✋ Moderate 🚇 Staroměstská 🚃 17, 18 to Lávka

STAROMĚSTSKÁ RADNICE

See pages 32–33.

STAROMĚSTSKÉ NÁMĚSTÍ (OLD TOWN SQUARE)

As early as the 12th century the Old Town Square was a thriving market place. Merchants from all over Europe conducted their business here and in the Ungelt (► 60), a courtyard behind the Týn Church. The square was also a place of execution: among the victims were the Hussite rebel Jan Želivský and the 27 Protestant noblemen who died here following the Battle of the White Mountain in 1620 (they are commemorated by white crosses set in the pavement in front of Old Town Hall). Jan Hus, the father of Czech Protestantism, died in Constance, but his monument, a stark sculpture by Ladislav Šaloun (1915), stands in the centre of the square.

Today the Old Town Square is full of outdoor cafés, and at Easter and Christmas, it is transformed into a marketplace, with wooden huts selling all kinds of small crafts and Czech delicacies. Crowds mill around under the Astronomical Clock on the Old Town Hall (► 32–33) as it performs its mesmerizing hourly routine. But the square's chief glory is its architecture: the Renaissance and baroque façades of the houses conceal Gothic substructures and Romanesque cellars. The beautiful rococo embellishments on the Golz-Kinsky Palace, dating from 1765 (No 12 east side) are by Kilián Dientzenhofer. Franz Kafka went to school here in the 1890s. Directly in front of the Týn Church, the ribbed vaulting in the 14th-century Týn School arcade has survived.

🚩 134 C4 ⊠ Staroměstské náměstí, Staré Město 🍴 Cafés (££), restaurants (£££) 👟 Free 🚇 Staroměstská

STAVOVSKÉ DIVADLO (ESTATES THEATRE)

This famous theatre was built between 1781 and 1783 for Count F A Nostitz-Rieneck, who wanted to raise the cultural profile of the city. On 29 October 1787, the count had his wish when Mozart's opera *Don Giovanni* received its world première here after being rejected by the conservative Viennese theatre managers. 'The people of Prague understand me', the composer said after conducting the performance from the piano. In 1984 Miloš Forman shot the relevant scenes of his Oscar-winning film *Amadeus* in the

auditorium, drawing attention to the need for renovation. That work was completed in the 1990s.

www.narodnidivadlo.cz

🚩 134 D4 ⊠ Ovocný trh 1, Staré Město ☎ 224 902 231
🕐 For concerts and tours
👟 Free 🍴 Café (££)
🚇 Můstek

UNGELT

From the 12th to the 18th centuries, this courtyard behind the Týn Church was a centre of commerce, where merchants paid *ungelt*, or customs duties. There was also a hostel offering accommodation for travellers here. The complex of 18 buildings

dates from the 16th century onwards and has been restored as shops, hotels and offices. The Granov Palace (Granovský palác), built on the northern side of the square for a wealthy tax collector in 1560, is one of the most distinguished Renaissance buildings in Prague, with sgraffito depicting biblical and classical themes and a magnificent loggia.

✠ 135 C5 ✉ Týnský dvůr, Staré Město 🍴 Restaurant in Hotel Ungelt (£££); others (££) 🚇 Staroměstská

Hradčany, Malá Strana and Beyond

Hradčany, on the left bank of Vltava River, is dominated by 16th-century Prague Castle, primarily a tourist attraction with its cathedral, museums and galleries, but also a seat of government – the President and his ministers have their offices here. Nowadays, many of the mansions and palaces are used as government offices, museums or even restaurants, and monuments in the surrounding neighbourhoods bear witness to the influence of Mozart and Joseph Stalin.

Malá Strana (Lesser Quarter), beneath the castle, is distinguished by the green of its gardens and orchards, created in the 17th century by the aristocrats who built their palaces here. The film *Amadeus*, which chronicles the life of Mozart, was filmed here, using the 18th-century architecture to create an illusion of Vienna at that time. Crowning Malostranské náměstí is the majestic, green-domed Church of St Nicholas. Nearer the Vltava, the small neighbourhood of Na Kampě is perfect for an evening stroll.

The area of Smíchov lies to the south, its highlights being the Mozart Museum and concerts that take place at Villa Bertramka.

The districts of Letná, Bubeneč and Holešovice spread out to the north and east where you'll find an art museum, a giant Metronome and a few relics from Prague's Communist past.

BERTRAMKA (MOZART MUSEUM)

This hillside villa, the home of the soprano Josefina Dušek and her composer husband František, was where Wolfgang Amadeus Mozart stayed on his visits to Prague in 1787 and 1791. Although the house was badly damaged by fire in 1873, the rooms Mozart occupied have survived and now contain a small exhibition on the composer and his happy relationship with the Bohemian capital. The most highly valued items, apart from the manuscripts, are his harpsichord and a lock of his hair. But his presence can best be felt in the lovely garden. It was here, on the night of 28 October 1787, that Mozart dashed off the sublime overture to his opera, *Don Giovanni*, just one night before the première was given in the Estates Theatre (➤ 59).

www.bertramka.cz

✚ 136 D2 ✉ Mozartova 169, Smíchov, Praha 5 ☎ 257 316 753 🕓 Apr–Oct daily 9–6; Nov–Mar daily 9.30–4 🖐 Inexpensive 🍴 Café (£) 🚇 Anděl then tram 9 to Bertramka ❓ Concerts Wed and Sat 5pm (held outside in summer)

BÍLÁ HORA (WHITE MOUNTAIN)

In the space of an hour, on 8 November 1620, the Catholic Habsburg army routed the Czech Protestants on this hillock

outside Prague, deciding the fate of Bohemia for the next 300 years. The battle is commemorated by a small stone monument and the Church of Our Lady of Victories (1704–14).

Also in the park is the Renaissance hunting lodge Letohrádek hvědza (Star Castle), built between 1555 and 1557 by Ferdinand of Tyrol. The castle now contains exhibitions devoted to the work of the writer Alois Jirásek and the painter Mikoláš Aleš.

www.hrady.cz

➕ 132 B1 (off map) ✉ Obora Hvezda 160 00, Liboc, Praha 6 ☎ Castle: 235 357 938 🕔 Castle: May–Sep Tue–Sun 10–6; Apr, Oct Tue–Sun 10–5 🎫 Castle: inexpensive 🚌 8, 22 to Vypich, or bus 179 from Petřín

BŘEVNOVSKÝ KLÁŠTER (BŘEVNOV MONASTERY)

There has been a monastery in Břevnov since AD993, although the present baroque complex, designed by Christoph and Karl Dientzenhofer, dates from 1708 to 1745. The monastery has now been returned to the Benedictines. The remarkable St Margaret's Church, built over a Romanesque crypt, has stunning oval ceiling frescoes by Johann Steinfels, depicting scenes from the legend of St Adalbert, while the Theresian Hall has a magnificent painting of Blessed Günther by Kosmas Assam.

www.brevnov.cz

➕ 132 B1 (off map) ✉ Markétská 28, Břevnov, Praha 6 ☎ 220 406 111 🕔 Apr–Oct Sat–Sun 10, 2, 4; Nov–Mar Sat–Sun 10, 2 or by appointment 🎫 Moderate 🚌 22, 25

ČERNÍNSKÝ PALÁC (ČERNÍN PALACE)

So much stone was used in the construction of this vast palace, with a façade stretching the entire length of Loretánské náměstí (135m/443ft), that it was said that the builders were being paid by the cubic metre. Certainly the palace's original owner, Count Jan Černín of Chudenice, Imperial Ambassador to Venice, spared no expense on the interior decoration – the work of the sculptor, Matthias Braun and the painter Václav Reiner, among others. In 1948, 20 years after the palace was acquired by the Ministry of Foreign Affairs, Jan Masaryk, son of the founder of Czechoslovakia and the only non-Communist member of the government, fell to his death from an upper floor window into the courtyard below. It is now widely believed that Masaryk was murdered on the orders of Stalin.

🚹 132 C2 ⊠ Loretánské náměstí 5, Hradčany ☎ None Ⓒ Not open to public 🚌 22, 23

CHRÁM SVATÉHO MIKULÁŠ
See pages 22–23.

HRADČANSKÉ NÁMĚSTÍ
(HRADČANY SQUARE)

This is a square of stunning Renaissance and baroque façades. The Archbishop's Palace (No 16) was given its eye-catching rococo face-lift in 1764 by the architect Johan Wirch, and is adorned with the family crest of Archbishop Antonín Příchovský.

Across the square is the Renaissance Schwarzenberg Palace, which features what is considered the best sgraffito in Prague. The yellow-fronted Tuscany Palace (No 5), once owned by the Duke of Tuscany, dates from 1689 to 1691. Jaroslav Bořita of Martinitz gave his name to the handsome palace at No 8.

✚ 132 C3 ✉ Hradčanské náměstí, Hradčany 🍴 Café (£) 🚌 22

KATEDRÁLA SVATÉHO VÍTA
See pages 26–27.

KLÁŠTER SVATÉHO JIŘÍ
(ST GEORGE'S CONVENT AND BASILICA)
St George's Convent houses the National Gallery's collection of Czech Mannerist and baroque art, and adjoining it is the Basilica, one of the oldest religious foundations in Prague, dating back to 920 and reconstructed in its present Romanesque form after a fire in 1142 (the baroque façade is a 17th-century addition). To the right of the entrance to the crypt is the painted wooden tomb of the founder, Prince Vratislav.

The exhibition in the convent begins with a display of Mannerist works by artists from the court of the Emperor Rudolph II: Bartholomeus Spranger, Hans von Aschen, Benedikt Wurzelbauer and Adrian de Vries – don't miss his superb sculpture *Stepping Horse* (c1610). The National Gallery's outstanding collection of baroque paintings and sculptures can be found on the first floor. Many of the Bohemian and Silesian artists exhibited here played a key role in beautifying Prague's churches and monasteries in the 17th and 18th centuries. They include Škreta, impressively

represented by altarpieces, portraits and easel paintings, Peter Brandl, Václav Reiner and the sculptor Matthias Braun. Look out for some outstanding portraits by Jan Kupecký, notably *Self-Portrait with Wife* (after 1725) and Ignaz Platzer, a master of the rococo whose commissions included the decoration of the Church of St Nicholas in the Lesser Quarter.

✚ 132 B4 ✉ Jirské námsětí 33, Hradčany
☎ 224 373 368; 224 372 434 🕐 Tue–Sun 9–5
✋ Moderate 🍴 Café (£), restaurants (££–£££)
near by 🚌 22, 23 to Pražský hrad

KOSTEL PANNY MARIE VÍTĚZNÉ
(OUR LADY VICTORIOUS)

The chief attraction of this 17th-century church is a wax effigy of the infant Jesus, known by its Italian name 'Il Bambino di Praga'. Believed to have miracle-working properties, the statue was brought from Spain in 1628 by Polxena of Lobkowicz and presented to the Carmelite nuns.

www.pragjesu.info

🚩 133 D5 ✉ Karmelitská 9, Malá Strana ☎ 257 533 646 🕐 Museum: Mon–Sat 9.30–5.30, Sun 1–6. Church: Mon–Sat 8.30–7, Sun 8.30–8 📳 Free 🚊 12, 22, 23

KOSTEL SVATÉHO TOMÁŠE
(ST THOMAS'S CHURCH)

This church was established for the Order of the Augustinian hermits by King Wenceslas II, 1285, at the same time as the neighbouring Augustinian monastery, and has undergone many reincarnations over the centuries, the latest between 1723 and 1731 after it was damaged by lightning. The ceiling is covered in frescoes by Václav Reiner depicting the life of St Augustine and, in the dome, the legend of St Thomas. Amazingly, Reiner completed the work in just two years. Other distinguished artists, including Karel Škréta and the sculptor Ferdinand Brokoff, also contributed to the décor, while the paintings (copies) over the high altar, of St Thomas and St Augustine, were commissioned from Rubens (the originals are now in the Šternberský palác ➤ 34–35).

🚩 133 C5 ✉ Josefská 8, Malá Strana ☎ 257 532 675 🕐 Daily. Mass in English Sun 11am 📳 Free 🚇 Malostranská 🚊 12, 22, 23

KRÁLOVSKÁ ZAHRADA (ROYAL GARDENS)

These delightful gardens with wonderful views were laid out in 1534 in the style of the Italian Renaissance. Four years later, work began on the Belvedere, the handsome summer house presented by Ferdinand I to his wife, Anna Jagiello. A magnificent arcaded building with a copper roof resembling an upturned ship's hull, it was completed in 1564 by Paolo Della Stella, who also designed the mythological reliefs. The palace is now used for exhibitions. The sgraffitoed Ball Game Hall at the eastern end of the gardens is the work of the Czech architect, Bonifaz Wohlmut, and was given its name by courtiers who played a form of tennis here. Tulips grow in the gardens every spring – another reminder

of Ferdinand I, who introduced the flower to Europe from Turkey in the 16th century. Near the entrance is the Lion's Court, once a menagerie exhibiting bears, panthers, tigers and other wild beasts.

🕂 133 B5 ✉ Královsky letohrádek, Hradčany ☎ Castle information: 224 373 368 🕓 Gardens: Apr–Oct daily 10–6; gardens on the bastion and gardens on the terrace open all year 👋 Free 🍴 Restaurant (£££) 🚌 22, 23

LAPIDÁRIUM

Located in an art nouveau pavilion in Výstaviště (the Exhibition Ground), this is a fascinating review of Czech sculpture from the 11th to the 19th centuries, with explanatory leaflets in English and other languages. One of the earliest exhibits is a beautifully ornamented column from the crypt of the 11th-century Basilica of St Vitus; other displays include the Krocín fountain, a remarkable Renaissance monument which used to stand on Old Town Square, and the 9m-high (30ft) Bear Gate, also known as the Slavata Portal, which once adorned a beautiful baroque garden in the Smíchov district. Ferdinand Brokoff's statues of St Ignatius and St Francis Xavier, now adorning the Charles Bridge, are copies. The originals exhibited here were torn down in the floods of 1890.

🕂 140 C3 ✉ Výstaviště 422, Holešovice, Praha 7 ☎ 233 375 636 🕓 Tue–Fri 12–6, Sat–Sun 10–6 👋 Inexpensive 🍴 Cafés (£) 🚇 Vltavská then tram 5 or 12 to Výstaviště 🚌 5, 12, 17

LENNONOVA ZED' (LENNON WALL)

Opposite the French embassy on Velkopřevoske náměstí, Kampa Island in Malá Strana, this stretch of wall was painted with democratic and pacifist graffiti following John Lennon's death in 1980. A game of cat-and-mouse ensued between police and artists as the wall was continually whitewashed and repainted. After the Velvet Revolution it was allowed to remain, at the request of the French ambassador.

✚ 133 D6 ✉ Velkopřevoské náměstí, Malá Strana 🚌 12, 27, 57

LORETA

See pages 28–29.

MALOSTRANSKÉ NÁMĚSTÍ (LESSER TOWN SQUARE)

The former market square of Malá Strana dates from 1257. Looming over the charming ensemble of baroque buildings is St Nicholas's Church and former Jesuit College (➤ 22–23). Many of the arcaded houses have now been converted into cafés and restaurants.

The centrepiece of the square is the attractive Renaissance Town Hall (1617–22) on the eastern side. Next door is the house At the Flavins, with a colourful fresco of the Annunciation.

✚ 132 C5 ✉ Malostranské náměstí, Malá Strana 🍴 Cafés (£), restaurants (££–£££) 🚇 Malostranská 🚌 12, 22

MALTÉZSKÉ NÁMĚSTÍ (MALTESE SQUARE)

This neighbourhood has been associated with the Order of the Knights of Malta since 1169. At the corner of Lázeňská is the former convent of the Order – Maltese crosses can still be seen on the main door and under the roof. Two impressive Gothic towers stand guard over the entrance to the Church of Our Lady Below the Chain, where a painting by Karel Škréta, decorating the main altar, depicts the victory of the Maltese Knights over the Turks at Lepanto in 1571. At the southern end of the square are two grand palaces: the brilliant pink-and-white Palais Turba, now the Japanese Embassy, and the ornate Nostitz Palace (open for chamber music concerts), which belongs to the Dutch Embassy.

✚ 133 D5 ✉ Maltézské náměstí, Malá Strana 🍴 Restaurants (£££) 🚌 12, 22, 23 to Malostranské náměstí

NÁRODNÍ TECHNICKÉ MUZEUM
(NATIONAL TECHNICAL MUSEUM)

The vast, glass-roofed central hall is the main attraction of this museum, with its exhibition on the history of transport, featuring a fascinating array of more than 500 types of vehicles, machines and models. Suspended from the ceiling is the skeleton of an early powered glider dating from 1905 and J Kašpar's Bleriot-XI monoplane of 1910. A magnificent steam engine and tender, built in Prague for the Austrian State Railways in 1911, dwarfs everything else in the locomotives exhibition, and a wonderful collection of early automobiles starts with an 1893 Benz 'Viktoria'. Later automobile models on show include some 1970s and '80s

Skoda coupés. The Czechs' own Skoda Works are represented by a wood-upholstered fire engine from 1928. Among the 40,000 items displayed elsewhere in the museum are a variety of film cameras, clocks, astrolabes, sextants, phonographs and much else besides. Visits to the simulated mining gallery are by guided tour only.

www.ntm.cz

✚ 140 F2 ✉ Kostelní 42, Holešovice, Praha 7 ☎ 220 399 111 🕐 Tue–Fri 9–5, Sat–Sun 10–6

🎟 Inexpensive 🚇 Vltavská, Hradčanksá 🚊 1, 8, 25, 26 to Letenské náměstí

NERUDOVA

This street honours Pavel Neruda (1834–91), whose short stories capture perfectly the small-town atmosphere of 19th-century Prague, and who was born at No 47. It's a steep climb to the top – Nerudova was originally called Spur Street after the brake which was applied to coaches on their descent. On your way you will see some wonderful 18th-century house signs (numbers were not introduced until the 1770s). Look out for The Red Eagle (No 6), The Three Fiddles (No 12), The Golden Cup (No 16), The Golden Horseshoe (No 34), The Green Lobster (No 43), the Two Suns (No 47) and the White Swan (No 49). Two magnificent baroque mansions, the Thun-Hohenstein Palace (No 20) and the Morzin Palace (No 5) are now the Italian and Romanian embassies. Nerudova leads eventually to Prague Castle, a wonderful vantage point from which to view the city.

✠ 132 C4 ✉ Nerudova, Malá Strana ⑪ Cafés (£), restaurants (££–£££)
🚌 12, 20, 22, 23 to Malostranské náměstí

NOVÝ SVĚT (NEW WORLD)

Nový Svět is a country lane of cottages dating back to the 17th century. Look out for U zletého noha (At the Golden Griffin, No 1), where astronomers Tycho Brahe and Johannes Kepler lived and U zlaté hrušky (At the Golden Pear, No 3), now a fine restaurant.
www.uzlatehrusky.cz

➕ 132 B2 ✉ Nový Svět, Hradčany 🍴 Restaurant (£££) 🚌 22, 23 to Pohořelec

PETŘÍNSKÉ SADY (PETŘÍN HILL)

Petřín Hill, where pagans once made sacrifices to their gods and medieval monarchs executed their enemies, is today a restful haven with panoramic views of the city. Crowning the summit is the baroque Church of St Lawrence; the ceiling fresco here depicts the founding of an earlier church in 991 on the site of a pagan shrine. The 60m-high (197ft) Observation Tower, modelled on the Eiffel Tower in Paris, was built for the Jubilee Exhibition of 1891, along with the Mirror Maze and a diorama depicting a battle between the Czechs and the Swedes for control of the Charles Bridge in 1648. Encircling the hill is the Hunger Wall, built in 1360 by Charles IV to provide employment in a time of famine. Further down the hill is the Observatory and Planetarium.

➕ 133 F5 ✉ Petřínské sady, Malá Strana ☎ Tower: 257 320 112 ✉ All attractions: May–Aug daily 10–10; Apr, Sep 10–7; Oct 10–6; Nov–Mar Sat–Sun 10–5 🍴 Restaurant (£££) 🚠 Funicular 🚌 6, 9, 12, 22, 23 to Újezd

PRAŽSKÝ HRAD

See pages 30–31.

ŠTERNBERSKÝ PALÁC

See pages 34–35.

STRAHOVSKÝ KLÁŠTER

See pages 36–37.

a walk through the Lesser Quarter

From Malostranská metro station take Valdštejnská to Valdštejnské náměstí.

Valdštejnské náměstí is named after the Imperial commander, Albrecht von Valdstein, whose palace straddles the east side (► 80–81). Behind the Ledebour Palace (No 3) are two attractive terraced gardens (open to the public), hugging the slopes below Prague Castle.

Take Tomásská to Malostranské náměstí. Walk along the east side of the square to Karmelitská.

Before crossing to Malostranské náměstí, stop to admire Dientzenhofer's baroque church, St Thomas's (► 68). The lower part of the square was once the site of a gallows and pillory. Now café tables spill onto the pavement outside the Town Hall.

Leave the square by Karmelitská and continue past Tržiště to the Church of Our Lady Victorious (► 68) which contains the celebrated statue of Il Bambino di Praga.

On the corner of Tržiště you pass the Vrtba Palace, which has a delightful terraced garden, constructed around 1720.

Cross Karmelitska and turn left down Harantova. Walk through Maltézské náměstí (➤ 73) and turn right onto Velkopřevorské náměstí, which leads down to the river.

Beyond the Lennon Wall (➤ 72) and the approach to the Vltava is a little bridge crossing the Čertovka (Devil's Stream). On your left is the waterwheel of the Grand Prior's Mill, which, in common with much of the area, belonged to the Order of the Knights of Malta.

Turn right and follow the river to most Legií, where you can catch a tram back to the centre.

Distance 2km (1 mile)
Time 2hours without stops
Start point 🅜 Malostranská ✚ 135 B6
End point most Legií ✚ 133 F6 🚊 6, 9, 22, 23
Lunch U Malého Glena (£££) ✉ Karmelitská 23, Malá Strana
☎ 257 531 717; www.malyglen.cz

TROJSKÝ ZÁMEK (TROJA CHÂTEAU)

Count Wenceslas Šternberg cut a swathe through the royal hunting grounds in order to build his version of Versailles at Stromovka. Work began on the striking red-and-white château around 1679. The palace itself is modelled on an Italian villa, but after the death of the original architect, responsibility for the project passed into the hands of a Frenchman, Jean-Baptiste Mathey. To honour the architect's intentions, it is necessary to approach the château from the south, where the formal French garden, restored in the 1980s, leads to an elaborate staircase decorated with heroic statues representing the 'gigantomachia' – the epic struggle between the Gods of Olympus and the Titans. The château apartments now house 19th-century Czech paintings. Most of the ceiling paintings are by an Italian artist, Francesco Marchetti, but for the Grand Hall the count turned to the Flemish painter, Abraham Godyn. His frescoes are Šternberg's effusive tribute to his Habsburg masters, notably Leopold I, whose triumph over the Ottomans at the gates of Vienna is symbolized by a Turk tumbling from the painting.
www.ghmp.cz

➕ 140 B1 (off map) ✉ U Trojského zámku 1, Troja, Praha 7 ☎ 283 851 614
🕐 Apr–Oct Tue–Sun 10–6; Nov–Mar Sat–Sun 10–5 ✋ Moderate 🚌 Bus
112 from Nádraží Holešovice

VALDŠTEJNSKÝ PALÁC A SADY (WALLENSTEIN PALACE AND GARDENS)

The Imperial General, Albrecht of Wallenstein (1583–1634), was a swashbuckling figure who amassed a tremendous fortune before succumbing to a blow from the assassin's axe. High-walled gardens were laid out in front of the palace by Niccolo Sebregondi between 1624 and 1630. The ceiling of the triple-arched *salla terrena*, designed in the Italian Renaissance style by Giovanni

Pieronni, is decorated with scenes from the Trojan Wars. An avenue of bronze sculptures by Adam de Vries leads from the pavilion (these are copies: the originals were taken by the Swedes during the Thirty Years' War). At the far end of the garden is the Riding School, now an exhibition hall.

www.senat.cz

✚ 133 C6 ✉ Valdštejnské náměstí 4, Malá Strana ☎ 257 071 111
🕐 Sat–Sun 10–5 ✋ Free Ⓜ Malostranská 🚊 12, 20, 22, 23

VELETRŽNÍ PALÁC
See pages 40–41.

VÝSTAVÍŠTĚ – MORSKÝ SVĚT
(EXHIBITION GROUND – SEAWORLD)

The Exhibition Ground in Letná Park dates from 1891 and has splendid art nouveau pavilions. Here also is Seaworld, a vast exhibition space devoted to the life of the deep. The 50 tanks, contain more than 150 species of salt and freshwater fish and a coral cave, constructed with American help in 2003. State-of-the-art technology replicates the natural environment with sensitized lighting, whilewater pumps simulate high and low tides.
www.morsky-svet.cz

✚ 140 C3 ✉ Výstavište, Holešovice, Praha 7 🚌 5, 12, 14, 15, 17 to Výstaviště

ZLATÁ ULIČKA (GOLDEN LANE)

This row of colourful little cottages, built hard against the walls of Prague Castle, originally provided homes for the archers of the Castle Guard. During the 17th century the palace goldsmiths moved into the area, giving the street its present name. Golden Lane gradually fell into decline and was little better than a slum when Franz Kafka was living with his sister at No 22 during the winter of 1916–17. Today souvenir shops occupy the cottages.

✚ 133 B5 ✉ Zlatá ulička, Pražský hrad, Hradčany ⏰ Apr–Oct daily 9–5; Nov–Mar daily 9–4 ✋ Inexpensive 🍴 Cafés (£) 🚇 Malostranská 🚌 22

Josefov Area

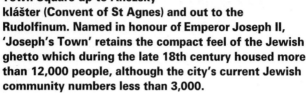

Josefov, the Old Jewish Quarter, is a compact area that stretches from Old Town Square up to Anežský klášter (Convent of St Agnes) and out to the Rudolfinum. Named in honour of Emperor Joseph II, 'Joseph's Town' retains the compact feel of the Jewish ghetto which during the late 18th century housed more than 12,000 people, although the city's current Jewish community numbers less than 3,000.

Like the Marais in Paris, Prague's Jewish quarter is now a neighbourhood of high rents, exclusive shops and expensive restaurants. Dominating the area are the beautiful Starý židovský hřbitov (Old Jewish Cemetery) and Staronová synagogá (Old-New Synagogue). On Maiselova Street you will find more synagogues and near to Pařížská třída (Paris Boulevard) is the Spanish Synagogue.

ANEŽSKÝ KLÁŠTER
(ST AGNES CONVENT)

The convent was founded in 1234 by Agnes, sister of King Wenceslas I. St Agnes introduced the Order of Poor Clares into Bohemia and was the first abbess. Completed by the end of the 14th century and sacked by the Hussites in the 15th, the convent was eventually dissolved in 1782. Restoration was completed in the 1990s. The most impressive building is the Church of the Holy Saviour, an outstanding example of early Gothic architecture. Look out for the capitals, highly decorated with reliefs showing the rulers of the Přemyslid dynasty. During restoration, the burial place of some of these kings and queens was unearthed, including the tomb of King Wenceslas in the Church of St Francis (which is now used as a concert venue).

The convent houses an exhibition of medieval art from Bohemia and Central Europe. Among the highlights are works by two artists from the reign of Charles IV: the Master of the Vyšší Brod Altar and Master Theodoric, whose lustrous portraits of the saints were intended for the chapel of Karlštejn Castle.

✚ 134 B4 ✉ U milosrdných 17, Josefov ☎ 224 810 628
🕐 Tue–Sun 10–6 💷 Moderate
🚇 Staroměstská, Náměstí Republiky 🚊 5, 17, 14, 26

EXPOZICE FRANZE KAFKY
(FRANZ KAFKA EXHIBITION)

A sculpted relief marks the site of the house where
Franz Kafka was born in 1883. Only the doorway of
the original building, At the Tower, remains
following a fire in 1887. Kafka's love-hate
relationship with Prague is reflected in his novels
The Trial and *The Castle*, where the city's
menacing presence looms over the characters.
Kafka died in 1924. A photographic exhibition of his
life can be found on the ground floor.

✚ 134 C3 ✉ Náměstí Franze
Kafky 3, Staré Město ☎ 222 321
675 ⏰ Tue–Fri 10–6, Sat 10–5
✋ Inexpensive 🍴 Café (£),
restaurants (££–£££) near by
Ⓜ Staroměstská

JOSEFOV

See pages 24–25.

KLAUSOVÁ SYNAGOGA
(KLAUSEN SYNAGOGUE)

A number of religious schools and other buildings
known as *klausen* were cleared away after the
great fire of 1689 to make way for this early
baroque synagogue. The fine interior, with barrel-
vaulted roof, stuccoed ceiling ornamentation and
stained-glass windows, has been restored and now
contains an exhibition on local Jewish customs and
traditions, including old Hebrew manuscripts and
prints, beautifully worked Torah ornaments, skull
caps embroidered in satin and velvet, bronze
Hanukkah lamps and a curious wooden alms box

(c1800) with a supplicating hand and arm. The marble Holy Ark, made in 1696 at the expense of Samuel Openheim, has also been restored.

✚ 134 C3 ✉ U starého hřbitova 3a, Josefov ☎ Jewish Museum: 222 317 191 🕐 Apr–Oct Sun–Fri 9–6; Nov–Mar Sun–Fri 9–4.30. Closed Sat and Jewish hols ✋ Moderate 🚇 Staroměstská 🚌 17, 18

KOSTEL SVATÉHO MIKULÁŠ (ST NICHOLAS'S CHURCH)

This beautifully proportioned baroque masterpiece was designed by the prolific architect Kilián Dientzenhofer in 1732 and completed three years later. (The sculptures of saints are by Antonín Braun.) St Nicholas's stands on the site of a much older Gothic church. When, in the spirit of the Enlightenment, the Emperor Joseph II evicted the Benedictines later in the 18th century, on the grounds that they were not performing a useful function, the church was used as a warehouse and fell into disrepair. It was saved during World War I when the commander of the occupying garrison invited local artists to restore Kosmas Asam's frescoes of saints Nicholas and Benedict in the dome. In other respects the building lacks the exuberance of baroque ornamentation.

Since 1920 St Nicholas has belonged to the Czech Reformed (Hussite) Church and is regularly used for concerts; the church has a 2,500-pipe organ.

✚ 134 C4 ✉ Staroměstské náměstí, Staré Město 🕐 Mon 12–4, Tue–Sat 10–4, Sun 10.30 (Mass), 12–3, also for concerts ✋ Free 🍴 Cafés (£), restaurants (££–£££) near by 🚇 Staroměstská

MAISELOVA SYNAGOGA (MAISEL SYNAGOGUE)

Originally a Renaissance temple, built in 1591 for Mayor Mordechai Maisel, financier to Emperor Rudolph II, the synagogue has a beautifully restored interior, which preserves some of the 16th-century stone carving.

The building now houses an exhibition of sacred religious objects, including items associated with the Torah. This consists of the five books of Moses, handwritten on rolls of parchment by scribes. By tradition the rollers would be elaborately decorated with filials, shields and crowns, superbly wrought in silver or brass and often gilded or encrusted with jewels. Examples of the richly embroidered mantles in which the Torah was wrapped are also on display in the synagogue, along with other items. But the most unusual exhibit is an enormous glass beaker, made between 1783 and 1784 for the Prague Burial Society and painted with a procession of men and women dressed in funereal black.

✚ 134 C3 ✉ Maiselova 10, Josefov ☎ Jewish Museum: 222 317 191
🕐 Apr–Oct Sun–Fri 9–6; Nov–Mar 9–4.30. Closed Sat and Jewish hols
✋ Moderate 🚇 Staroměstská 🚋 17, 18

MUZEUM UMĚLECKOPRŮMYSLOVÉ (MUSEUM OF DECORATIVE ARTS)

Once housed in the Rudolfinum, the museum moved to Josef Schulz's neo-Renaissance building in 1901, and boasts a rich collection of Czech and European applied arts. The collection of Bohemian glass dates back to the Renaissance and is outstanding, as are Venetian and medieval exhibits. There are selections of Meissen and Sèvres porcelain, exquisite majolica tableware from Urbino and Delft and beautifully inlaid cabinets, bureaux and escritoires, from baroque to Biedermeier. The museum shop sells a wide range of publications and souvenirs.

www.upm.cz

✚ 134 C3 ✉ 17 listopadu 2, Josefov ☎ 251 093 111 🕐 Tue 10–7, Wed–Sun 10–6 ✋ Inexpensive 🍴 Café (£) 🚇 Staroměstská 🚋 17, 18

NÁMĚSTÍ JANA PALACHA (JAN PALACH SQUARE)

'Red Army Square' was renamed after the 1989 Velvet Revolution in honour of Jan Palach, the 21-year-old philosophy student who burned himself to death in January 1969 as a protest against the Soviet occupation of Czechoslovakia. The authorities were unmoved but more than 800,000 people joined the funeral procession to Olšanské cemetery, where his remains were laid to rest. On the east side of the square is the philosophy building of Charles University, where Palach attended lectures: on the lower left-hand corner of the façade is a small bronze death mask by Olbran Zoubek.

✚ 134 C2 ✉ Náměstí Jana Palacha, Josefov ✋ Free 🍴 Café (£) near by
🚇 Staroměstská 🚌 17, 18

OBŘADNÍ SÍŇ (CEREMONIAL HALL)

The former Ceremonial Hall of the Prague Burial Society was once used for Jewish burial rites. It now houses a permanent exhibition on Jewish customs and traditions, with particular emphasis on the themes of illness and death.

✚ 134 B3 ✉ U starého hřbitova, Josefov ☎ Jewish Museum: 222 317 191
✉ Apr–Oct Sun–Fri 9–6; Nov–Mar 9–4.30. Closed Sat and Jewish hols
🚇 Staroměstská ✋ Moderate
🚌 17, 18

PINKASOVA SYNAGOGA (PINKAS SYNAGOGUE)

First mentioned in 1492, this synagogue was founded by Rabbi Pinkas and enlarged in 1535. A women's gallery and council hall were added in the 17th century. Now a Holocaust memorial, its walls have been painstakingly painted with the names of the 77,297 Bohemian and Moravian Jews who perished in Nazi death camps during World War II. (The original paintings were erased by the Communists when they closed the building in 1968, ostensibly to prevent flood damage.) During excavations, a medieval ritual bath was discovered in the basement, evidence that the site was a Jewish place of worship long before the time of Rabbi Pinkas.

The upper floor of the synagogue houses a moving collection of drawings by some of the 15,000 children who were confined at the Terezín concentration camp. Mrs Friedl Dicker-Brandeis (1898–1944), an artist and graduate of the Bauhaus, organised art classes which functioned as a kind of therapy for the children: their drawings often depicted their transportation to Terezín, their memories of home and their dreams of returning to their families.

✚ 134 C3 ✉ Široká 3, Josefov ☎ Jewish Museum: 222 317 191
🕐 Apr–Oct Sun–Fri 9–6; Nov–Mar 9–4.30. Closed Sat and Jewish hols
✋ Moderate 🍴 Café (£), restaurant (££) near by 🚇 Staroměstská 🚌 17, 18

RUDOLFINUM

One of Prague's leading cultural venues, the Rudolfinum is also a fine example of neo-Renaissance architecture. It was designed by Josef Zítek and Josef Schulz in 1876 and named in honour of the Austrian crown prince, Rudolph of Habsburg. During World War II it was used as the German Army HQ and before that (1918–38) it housed the first Czechoslovak parliament. Concert-goers will come to know the Dvořák Hall, home of the Czech Philharmonic orchestra (chamber concerts and recitals are held in the 'small hall'). The Galerie Rudolfinum is used for art shows and events.

www.rudolfinum.cz

✚ 134 C3 ✉ Alšovo nábřeží 12, Josefov ☎ 227 059 227 ⓖ Gallery:
Tue–Sun 10–6 ✋ Moderate ⓜ Staroměstská 🚋 17, 18

STARONOVÁ SYNAGOGA (OLD-NEW SYNAGOGUE)

Founded around 1270, the Old-New Synagogue is the oldest in Europe and is still open for worship. A typical Gothic building with a double nave, its most unusual feature is the five-ribbed vaulting of the main hall, unique in Bohemian architecture. Other details to look out for are the stepped brick gables on the exterior, the grape clusters and vine leaf motifs above the entrance portal and the medieval furnishings, including stone pews. There are 13th-century  Gothic carvings in the tympanum above the Holy Ark, and the iron lattice enclosing the *almenor* or *bimah* (the tribune from where the Torah is read) dates from the late 15th century. During the sabbath (Saturday) service seven members of the congregation join in the reading. Suspended between two of the pillars is a large red flag embroidered with the Star of David and the traditional Jewish cap. It was presented to the community in 1648 by the Emperor Ferdinand in appreciation of its contribution to the Thirty Years' War.

✚ 134 C3 ✉ Červená 2, Josefov ◉ Apr–Oct Sun–Thu 9–6, Fri 9–5;
Nov–Mar Sun–Thu 9–4.30, Fri 9–2. Closed Sat and Jewish hols ✋ Moderate
🍴 Restaurant (££) near by ◉ Staroměstská 🚃 17, 18

STARÝ ŽIDOVSKÝ HŘBITOV (OLD JEWISH CEMETERY)

One of the oldest Jewish burial grounds in Europe, the Old Jewish Cemetery was founded in the early 15th century: the earliest grave, belonging to Rabbi Avigdor Kara, dates from 1439. There are approximately 12,000 tombstones sprouting obliquely from the earth like broken and decaying teeth. Beneath them lie more than 100,000 bodies, buried layer upon layer in the confined space. The cemetery closed in 1787. This was the last resting place of many prominent members of the Jewish community, including Rabbi Jehuda Löw (1609), legendary inventor of the Golem, the mayor and philanthropist Mordechai Maisel (1601) and the renowned scholar Rabbi David Openheim (1736). The earliest headstones are of sandstone and have plain inscriptions, but from the 17th century they are decorated with carved marble reliefs indicating the trade or status of the deceased – for example, a pair of scissors for a tailor.

✚ 134 C3 ✉ U starého hřbitova, Josefov ☎ Jewish Museum: 222 317 191
🕐 Apr–Oct Sun–Fri 9–6; Nov–Mar 9–4.30. Closed Sat and Jewish hols
✋ Moderate 🚇 Staroměstská 🚌 17, 18

Nové Město and Beyond

The New Town was founded in the 14th century and is now the commercial and administrative heart of the city with new, modern buildings rubbing shoulders with old. It fills the area from the avenues of Na příkopě and Národní south by the Vltava River down to the dramatic ramparts of Vyšehrad. East of this is Vinohrady, a leafy neighbourhood filled with restaurants and parks.

Even first-time visitors will probably have heard of Wenceslas Square or Václavské náměstí. To call it a square is misleading; it's actually a long boulevard that is crowned at the top by a massive statue of St Wenceslas on horseback, and the majestic National Museum. Both sides of the 'square' are

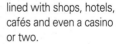

lined with shops, hotels, cafés and even a casino or two.

The Národní divadlo (National Theatre) and the Café Slavia, once the haunt of dissidents in communist times, are both highlights of Nové Město and are on Národní třída.

CHRÁM PANNY MARIE SNĚŽNÉ (OUR LADY OF THE SNOWS)

Founded in 1347 by Charles IV, Our Lady of the Snows was to have been the largest church in Prague – 40m (131ft) high and 110m (360ft) long – but the outbreak of the Hussite wars interrupted work on the building. In 1603 the completed choir was restored to the Franciscans and given a baroque face-lift and a new vaulted ceiling. All that remains of the 14th-century church are the crumbling pediment over the north gateway and the pewter font. The Franciscan Gardens are now a public park.

www.pms.ofm.cz

🔡 134 E4 ✉ Jungmannovo náměstí 18, Nové Město ☎ 224 916 100 🕓 Daily 7–7. Mass: Mon–Fri 7am, 8am and 6pm, Sat 8am and 6pm, Sun 9am, 10.15am, 11.30am and 6pm. Evening concerts: tickets at the door 🖐 Free 🔲 Můstek

DVOŘÁKA ANTONÍN MUZEUM (DVORAK MUSEUM)

This beautiful baroque mansion, built by Kilián Dientzenhofer between 1717 and 1720 for a prominant Czech nobleman, acquired its present name, Vila Amerika, in the 19th century – there was an eating house of that name near by. It is therefore entirely appropriate that the building now honours the composer of the 'New World' symphony, Antonín Dvořák (1841–1904). Unfortunately, the palatial interior, with partly restored frescoes by Johann Schlor, is not really suitable for such an intimate exhibition. The exhibits, spread over two floors, include autographed scores, photographs, busts and portraits, correspondence with fellow musicians (the composers Brahms and Tchaikovsky, and the German conductor Hans von Bulöw, were among Dvořák's friends and admirers) and a number of personal effects including his viola, Bible and spectacles. The first floor is also used for concerts.

www.nm.cz

✚ 138 B4 ✉ Ke Karlovu 20, Nové Město ☎ 224 918 013 ⏰ Tue–Sun 10–5 ✋ Inexpensive Ⓜ IP Pavlova 🚋 4, 10, 16, 22, 23

KOSTEL SVATÉHO CYRILA A METODĚJE (CHURCH OF SAINTS CYRIL AND METHODIUS)

A plaque on the bullet-scarred wall of this Orthodox cathedral commemorates the Free Czech paratroopers who died here on 18 June 1942, after taking part in the assassination of the Nazi Governor of Bohemia and Moravia, Reinhard Heydrich. Members of the Czech Orthodox community hid them in the crypt, but they were discovered, and committed suicide rather than fall into enemy hands. Saints Cyril and Methodius was designated a National Memorial to the victims of the Heydrich Terror.

www.pravoslavnacirkev.cz

✚ 138 A2 ✉ Resslova 9, Nové Město ☎ 224 920 686 ⏰ Apr–Oct Tue–Sun 10–5; Nov–Mar Tue–Sun 10–4. Crypt by appointment only ✋ Inexpensive Ⓜ Karlovo náměstí 🚋 4, 6, 10, 14, 16, 22, 23, 24

MUZEUM HLAVNÍHO MĚSTA PRAHY
(CITY OF PRAGUE MUSEUM)

One of the three historic buildings that make up the City of Prague Museum, Hlavni Budova na Florenci charts the history of the city and includes exhibits which range from the earliest times to the 20th century. Among the various household items on display are slippers, combs and a 14th-century wash-tub, as well as pottery and coins. The medieval craft guilds are represented in displays of tools, signs and seals, and by some fine examples of their workmanship, including a mural painting of 1406, originally executed for the House at the Golden Angel in Old Town Square. Weapons, model soldiers and cannons and the lock of the original Bethlehem Chapel door (➤ 46–47) are used to illustrate the Hussite period, and there is an impressive collection of statuary, notably a wooden *pietà* from the Týn Church (➤ 53) and a stone

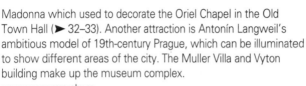

Madonna which used to decorate the Oriel Chapel in the Old Town Hall (➤ 32–33). Another attraction is Antonín Langweil's ambitious model of 19th-century Prague, which can be illuminated to show different areas of the city. The Muller Villa and Vyton building make up the museum complex.

www.muzeumprahy.cz

✛ 135 C8 ✉ Na poříčí 52, Karlín, Praha 8 ☎ 224 212 966 ⏰ Daily 9–9 ✋ Inexpensive 🚇 Florenc 🚌 8, 24

MUZEUM KOMUNISMU (MUSEUM OF COMMUNISM)

As a modern visitor to Prague it's all too easy to forget that for more than 40 years (1948–89) the Czech Republic was an occupied country within the Soviet bloc, a client state adhering to the prevailing Communist ideology. Through photographs, household ephemera, agricultural machinery, military hardware, propaganda posters, reproductions of bare food shelves and 'Young Pioneer' classrooms, the exhibition 'Dreams, Reality and Nightmare of Communism' is an intriguing introduction to life in a satellite Soviet state and a sobering reminder of what the Czech people had to endure. An interrogation room from the 1950s show-trial era is chillingly reproduced, and the persistent ring of a black telephone is a suitably eerie touch.

www.muzeumkommunismu.cz

✛ 135 D5 ✉ Savarin Palace, Na příkopě 10, Nové Město (first floor, same as casino) ☎ 224 212 966 ⏰ Daily 8am–9pm ✋ Moderate 🚇 Můstek

MUZEUM ALPHONSE MUCHY (MUCHA MUSEUM)

This museum allows you an opportunity to discover the work of one of the great masters of art nouveau, Alphonse Mucha (1860–1939). Mucha began his career in 1887, shortly after studying at the Academy of Arts in Munich, when he found work as a set painter and decorator in Vienna and Paris. His most famous early illustrations were the posters designed for the French actress Sarah Bernhardt. He settled in Prague in 1910, having spent several years teaching.

Other examples of his work can be seen in Obecní dům, the National Gallery and the Art and Industry Museum. The collection is a representative cross-section of works from the Mucha Foundation: paintings, drawings, lithographs, pastels, sculptures, photographs and personal memorabilia. The museum shop sells a range of souvenirs and gorgeous poster reproductions with the elegant Mucha motif.

www.mucha.cz

✚ 135 D5 ✉ Panská 7, Nové Město ☎ 221 451 333 ⏰ Daily 10–6 ✋ Moderate Ⓜ Můstek 🚌 5, 9 to Jindřišská

NA PŘÍKOPĚ (ON THE MOAT)

This busy, pedestrian-only street takes its name from the moat that once formed a boundary between the Old and New Towns. Today it is one of Prague's major shopping thoroughfares, with some compelling architecture from the late 19th century, when a number of major banking houses established their offices here. Particularly impressive is No 18–20. Actually two buildings connected by a bridge, it was designed by Osvald Polívka and completed in 1896. An earlier building, No 10 on the south side, was designed by Kilián Ignac Dienzenhofer in 1743 and served as a casino then as it does now. The colourful mosaics in the lunettes are from cartoons by the Czech artist Mikoláš Aleš.

✚ 135 D5 ✉ Na příkopě, Nové Město ✋ Free 🍴 Cafés (£), restaurants (££) Ⓜ Můstek, Náměstí Republiky

NÁRODNÍ DIVADLO (NATIONAL THEATRE)

Partly funded by public donations, the founding of a National Theatre in this striking building represented the re-emergence of Czech nationalism in the mid-19th century. The foundation stone was laid in 1848, and when the almost completed theatre was destroyed by fire in 1881, more money was raised and a second National Theatre was finished in just two years. The design by Josef Schulz closely followed Josef Zítek's original.

The decoration was entrusted to a group of artists who became known as 'the generation of the National Theatre'. The loggia facing Národní has five arcades decorated with lunette paintings by Josef Tulka, while the attic contains statues by Bohuslav Schnirch, Antonin Wagner and Josef Myslbek. The interior is even more resplendent: in the portrait gallery, Myslbek sculpted bronze busts of Smetana and other contributors to Czech opera and drama, and Mikoláš Aleš, Adolf Liebscher and František Ženíšek filled the foyers with paintings. The stage curtain depicting the story of the National Theatre is by Voitěch Hynais.

www.narodni-divadlo.cz

➕ 134 F2 ✉ Národní 2, Nové Město ☎ Box office: 224 901 377
🍴 Café-bar (££) 🚇 Národní třída 🚊 6, 9, 17, 18, 22, 23 to Národní divadlo
❓ Tours Sat–Sun 8.30–11am

NÁRODNÍ MUZEUM (NATIONAL MUSEUM)

This stolid neo-Renaissance building, crowned with a gilded dome, dominates Wenceslas Square. Serving up large but unimaginative helpings of natural history, mineralogy, palaeontology, zoology and anthropology, the museum is worth visiting for the richly decorated Ceremonial Hall and Pantheon. Statues of famous Czechs compete with historical wall paintings and allegories of Science, Art, Inspiration and Power, all commissioned from Bohemia's best 19th-century sculptors and painters.

www.nm.cz

⊞ 135 F6 ⊠ Václavské náměstí 68, Nové Město ☎ 224 497 111

🕓 May–Sep daily 10–6; Oct–Apr daily 9–5. Closed first Tue every month

✋ Moderate 🍴 Café (£) 🚇 Muzeum 🚌 11

OBECNÍ DŮM (MUNICIPAL HOUSE)

One of Prague's most engaging art nouveau monuments, Obecní dům was conceived as a community centre with concert halls, assembly rooms, offices and cafés. Antonín Balšánek and Osvald Polívka won a competition for the design and it was completed in 1911. Each of the rooms has its own character, but there is overall unity in the stained-glass windows, inlaid floors, wrought-iron work and walls of polished wood or marble. Scarcely a Czech artist of the period failed to contribute to the interiors. The Smetana Concert Hall was decorated by Karel Špillar and Ladislav Šaloun; Alphonse Mucha was responsible for the Mayor's Salon. Špillar's large mosaic, *Homage to Prague*, on the façade, is also impressive. **www.**obecnidum.cz

➕ 135 C5 ✉ Náměstí Republiky 5, Nové Město ☎ 222 002 127; 222 002 101 ✋ Tours: moderate 🍴 Café (£), restaurants (£££) 🚇 Náměstí Republiky 🚌 5, 14, 26 ❓ Temporary exhibitions

PAMÁTNÍK 17 LISTOPADU 1989

In an arcade between Wenceslas Square and the National Theatre is a small plaque commemorating the incident that sparked the Velvet Revolution in 1989. On 17 November a large crowd, made up predominantly of students, headed towards Wenceslas Square from Vyšehrad, where they had been marking the 50th anniversary of the Nazi occupation. When they reached Národní they were confronted by riot police who charged, leaving hundreds severely beaten. Actors and theatre employees immediately called a strike, which led ultimately to the formation of Civic Forum.

✠ 134 E3 ✉ Národní, Nové Město 👆 Free 🍴 Cafés (£), restaurants (££–£££) near by 🚇 Národní třída 🚊 6, 9, 18, 22, 23

POŠTOVNÍ MUZEUM (POSTAL MUSEUM)

This unusual museum boasts a colourful collection of postage stamps from Czechoslovakia, the Czech Republic and Europe. The backdrop is an exhibition on the history of communications in the region, using prints, old signs and other ephemera. There are also temporary exhibitions. The frescoes in the showroom are by the 19th-century artist, Josef Navrátil.

www.cpost.cz

✠ 135 B6 ✉ Nové mlyny 2, Nové Město ☎ 222 312 006 🕐 Tue–Sun 9–5 👆 Inexpensive 🚇 Náměstí Republiky 🚊 5, 8, 14

PRAŠNÁ BRÁNA (POWDER GATE)

Work began on this sturdy Gothic tower in 1475, but was halted eight years later when rioting forced the king to flee the city. It still lacked a roof when Josef Mocker was asked to complete it in the 1870s. The gate acquired its name in the 17th century, when it was used to store gunpowder. Before then its functions had been ceremonial: coronation processions began here before moving off towards St Vitus's Cathedral.

✠ 135 D5 ✉ Na příkopě, Nové Město ☎ 724 063 723 🕐 Apr–Oct daily 10–6 👆 Moderate 🚇 Náměstí Republiky 🚊 5, 14, 26

VÁCLAVSKÉ NÁMĚSTÍ

See pages 38–39.

VYŠEHRAD

The twin spires of Vyšehrad church are one of Prague's best known landmarks. The early history of this settlement is bound in legend surrounding the first dynasty of Czech rulers, the Přemyslids, who established a fortress on the rocky outcrop in the middle of the 10th century. Prince Vratislav II (1061–92) built a walled palace here, the Basilica of St Peter and St Paul and a chapter house. By the mid-12th century, Prague Castle began to take precedence, but Vyšehrad's value as a stronghold was noted by Charles IV, who reinforced the walls and made this the start of his coronation procession.

The elaborate Leopold Gate of 1670 leads into the main compound. Past St Martin's Rotunda is the Old Deanery, standing on the site of a Romanesque basilica. Little remains of the early palaces, although from the terrace on the fortified walls there are views of 'Libuše's bath', actually a Gothic guard tower, as well as splendid vistas across the Vltava Valley. In the middle of the palace gardens is a medieval well – the statues by Josef Myslbek were removed from the Palacky Bridge after being damaged during a bombardment in 1945. The Church of St Peter and St Paul has been rebuilt many times, most recently in neo-Gothic style by Josef Mocker. In a side chapel is a medieval panel painting of the Virgin of the Rains, dating from 1350. Vyšehrad cemetery was founded in 1860 as a burial ground for Czech national heroes: the composers Antonín Dvořák and Bedřich Smetana, the artist Alphonse Mucha and the writer Karel Čapek are all buried here.
www.praha-vysehrad.cz

✚ 138 E2 ✉ V pevnosti 5, Vyšehrad, Praha 2 ☎ 241 410 348 ⏰ Apr–Oct daily 9.30–6; Nov–Mar 9.30–5 🎟 Inexpensive 🚇 Vyšehrad 🚃 7, 8, 24 to Albertov

Excursions

There are any number of possible excursions from Prague, many within an hour or two's journey by train or car. The variety of scenery may come as a surprise, from the craggy uplands of Český ráj and the Krkonoše (Giant) Mountains to the woodland slopes of the Berounka Valley. Further south around Třeboň is a wetland area of lakes and carp-rearing ponds, an ideal habitat for water birds; and there are other surprises in store: a fairy-tale castle on an isolated hill top, a gloomy limestone cave with dripping stalactites, a charming Renaissance town hall at the centre of a busy market square. The elegant 19th-century resort of Karlovy Vary is famous for its hot mineral springs; Plzeň and České Budějovice are both centres of the brewing industry, and the vineyards of Mělník date back to the reign of Charles IV.

BRNO

The capital of Moravia and the second city of the Republic, Brno is famous for its Motorcycle Grand Prix and trade fairs, but it is also a lively cultural centre with a major university and several theatres (including the Reduta, where Mozart conducted his own compositions in 1767) and some interesting historical sights. Two Brno landmarks – the Špilberk fortress, which for centuries served as a Habsburg prison and is now the city museum, and the Gothic Cathedral of St Peter and St Paul – stand on adjacent hills. Below the cathedral is the Old Town. It's worth climbing the tower of the Old City Hall for the views. Notice the middle turret of the hall's Gothic portal, which is askew: according to the local legend, it was left deliberately crooked by the builder as an act of revenge on the burghers for not paying his wages in full.

www.brno.cz

✚ 141 D3 ✉ Informační služba, Radnická 8 ☎ 542 173 590 🕐 Town Hall: Apr–Sep daily 9–5. Castle: Tue–Sun 9–5 💷 Inexpensive 🍴 Cafés (£), restaurants (££) 🚊 Praha Hlavní nádraží ❓ Aug–Sep: International Motorcycling Championship

a drive around the Bohemian Uplands

Leave Prague, heading northwards on highway 608 to Bohdanovice, then take highway 9 through Libeznice.

Crossing the River Labe, there are views of the vineyards which cluster around the delightful hillltop town of Mělník (➤ 122–123).

Continue on highway 9 to Dubá.

On your way you will pass through Liběchov, which has a château dating from 1730.

Turn left onto the 260 to Úštěk.

The ruins of Hrádek Castle will appear on your left as you approach Úštěk. This charming town posseses an attractive elongated square of Gothic and Renaissance houses, as well as the 'birds' cottages' built like nests on rocky promontories by Italian labourers who constructed the railway in the mid-19th century.

Leave Úštěk on highway 260, travelling northwards. This scenic route crosses the forested Central Bohemian Heights (České středohoří), a designated area of natural beauty. At Malé Březno turn left onto highway 261.

The road now tracks between the River Labe and its sandstone cliffs to the industrial town of Ústí nad Labem. On a promontory south of Ústí you will pass Střekov Castle, with its round Gothic tower. It is said to have been the inspiration for Richard Wagner's opera *Tannhäuser*.

Continue on the 261.

Drive through the orchards and hop gardens of the Labe Valley to Litoměřice, an attractive medieval market town with two town halls (Gothic and Renaissance) as well as numerous baroque churches and town houses.

Cross the river and join highway E55 through Terezín (► 126–127) to return to Prague.

Distance 131km (81 miles)
Time 8 hours
Start/end point Střížkov, Praha 9
Lunch U Tomáše (£) ✉ Náměstí Míru 30, Mělník ☎ 206 627 357

ČESKÉ BUDĚJOVICE

This sedate old town was founded in 1265 by King Otokar II
Přemysl as a base from which to attack his enemies, the unruly
Vítkovec clan. During the Hussite Wars the mainly German
population remained royalist and stoutly defended the Catholic
cause. Commercially, the 16th century was a golden age as České
Budějovice exploited its precious silver deposits, but the economic
and social dislocation caused by the Thirty Years' War put an end
to this prosperity and in 1641 the town was ravaged by a terrible
fire which damaged or destroyed almost every building of
importance. This led to large-scale reconstruction, which accounts
for the mainly baroque appearance of today's town. The advent of
the railways in the 19th century brought industry to the region and
České Budějovice became the third largest city in the country after
Prague and Plzeň. Today it is best known for its beer.

The town's main square, náměstí Přemysla Otakara II, is one of
the largest in Europe: the Town Hall, a graceful building dating
from 1727 to 1730, the 13th-century Church of St Nicholas and the
lofty Černá Věž (Black Tower) are the main attractions. It's a climb
of 360 steps to the Tower's viewing gallery, but well worth it. A
few minutes' walk away is the old meat market (Masné krámy),
dating from 1564, now serving as a traditional beer hall. Visitors
who develop a taste for Budvar may like to sign up for a tour of
the famous brewery.

www.c-budejovice.cz

🚩 141 C4 ✉ Informační centrum: náměstí Přemysla Otakara II 2 ☎ 386 801
413. Brewery: 387 705 111 🕐 Brewery: daily 9–3, for group tours 🍴 Cafés
(£), restaurants (££) 🚆 Praha Hlavní Nádraží ❓ Aug: International
Agricultural Show

ČESKÝ KRUMLOV

Český Krumlov is simply ravishing. Surrounded by rolling
countryside and the wooded Šumava Hills, the old town – a
UNESCO World Heritage Site – nestles in a bend of the Vltava

River. For more than 600 years its fortunes were inseparable from those of the aristocratic families residing in the castle: the lords of Krumlov, the Rožmberks, the Eggenbergs and finally the Schwarzenbergs, who were not dispossessed until after World War II. The castle is part medieval fortress, part château, magnificently set on a clifftop overlooking the town, and boasting a unique bridge resembling an aqueduct, a picture gallery and the oldest private theatre in Europe. Guided tours include a visit to the Hall of Masks, a ballroom painted in 1748 with *trompe-l'oeil* figures of guests attending a masquerade. The houses of the Latrán, the area around the castle, were originally occupied by servants and court scribes. Buildings here include a 14th-century Minorite Monastery and the Eggenberg Brewery, which still makes its deliveries by horse and cart. Below the castle steps is the medieval former hospice and Church of St Jošt, now converted into private apartments.

The nucleus of the town is on the opposite bank of the Vltava. Prominent on náměstí Svornosti (the main square) is the Town Hall, with attractive arcades and vaulting. Vilém of Rožmberk is buried in the Gothic Church of St Vitus, which dates from 1439. The Latin School, now a music school and the former Jesuit College, now the Hotel Růže, are also worth a look.

www.ckrumlov.cz

🞢 141 B4 ✉ Tourist Service Rooseveltova 28 ☎ 380 712 853 🕐 Castle: Apr–May, Sep–Oct Tue–Sun 9–12, 1–4; Jul–Aug Tue–Sun 9–12, 1–5. Tower: Apr–Oct Tue–Sun 9–6 💰 Moderate 🍽 Cafés (£), restaurants (££) 🚆 Praha Hlavní nádraží (via České Budějovice) ❓ Mid-Jun: Five-Petal Rose Festival; Aug: International Music Festival

ČESKÝ ŠTERNBERK

Founded in 1242 on a sheer cliff above the Sázava River, the fortress home of the Šternberk family commands wonderful views of the valley. The castle was remodelled in the baroque style by Italian craftsmen between 1660 and 1670. The rococo Chapel of St Sebastian and the Yellow Room, with an elaborate stucco moulding by Carlo Bentano, are particularly beautiful. There is also a display of silver miniatures and a set of engravings on the staircase which depict scenes from the Thirty Years' War.

🔢 141 C3 ✉ Český Šternberk ☎ 317 855 101 🕐 Jul–Sep Tue–Sun 9–6; May Sat–Sun 9–4; Jun, Oct Tue–Sun 9–5; Nov–Mar Sat–Thu 9–4
✋ Moderate 🍴 Restaurant (££) 🚌 Bus from Roztyly metro

HRADEC KRÁLOVÉ

Hradec Králové has been the regional capital of Eastern Bohemia since the 10th century. A Hussite stronghold in the 15th century, the town later featured in the Austro-Prussian war of 1866 as the site of the Battle of Königgrätz. At the heart of the old town is an attractive square (actually triangular in shape) known as Žižkovo náměstí after the Hussite warrior, Jan Žižka, who is buried here. Overlooking the square is the 14th-century Cathedral of the Holy Spirit. The free-standing belfry (71.5m/235ft high) is known as the White Tower, and was added later. Just in front of the tower is a

handsome Renaissance town hall. The Jesuit Church of the Assumption, on the southern side of the square, has an attractive 17th-century interior. Two leading art nouveau architects, Osvald Polívka and Jan Kot, worked in Hradec Králové. Polívka designed the Gallery of Modern Art, while Kot was responsible for the Regional Museum of East Bohemia just outside the Old Town.
www.hradeckralove.org

🕂 141 D2 ✉ Hradec Králové ☎ Information: 495 534 482 🕔 Museum and Gallery: Tue–Sun 9–12, 1–5 🍴 Cafés (£), restaurants (££) 🚆 Praha Hlavní nádraží 🛈 Information centre: Gočárova třída 1225

KARLOVY VARY

According to legend, Charles IV was out hunting one day when one of his hounds tumbled into a hot spring and the secret of Karlovy Vary was out. In 1522 Dr Payer of Loket set out the properties of the waters in a medical treatise and their fame began to spread. By the end of the 16th century there were more than 200 spa buildings, but the town's present appearance dates mainly from the 19th century.

There are 12 hot mineral springs in all, housed in five colonnades. The best known (and the hottest) is the Vřídlo, at 72°C (161°F), which spurts to a height of 10m (33ft). The wrought-iron Sadová and the neo-Renaissance Mlýnská colonnades preserve something of their 19th-century atmosphere.

Besides the curative waters, Karlovy Vary is famous for another, more potent liquid: a herb liquer called *Becherovka* after the doctor who invented the recipe while working at the spa in the early 1700s. The area comes alive in summer, when there are concerts and festivals.
www.karlovyvary.cz

🕂 141 A2 ✉ Lázeňská 1 ☎ 353 224 097 🍴 Cafés (£), restaurants (££–£££) 🚆 Coach from Praha Florenc 🛈 May: opening of Spa Season; Jul: International Film Festival

KARLŠTEJN

Perched on a cliff above the Berounka River, Karlštejn was founded by Charles IV in 1348 as a treasury for the imperial regalia and his collection of relics. In the 19th century the fortress was remodelled in neo-Gothic style by Joseph Mocker. Rooms open to the public include the wood-panelled Audience Hall, the Luxembourg Hall and the Church of Our Lady, which has a fine timber ceiling and fragments of 14th-century fresco painting. The magnificent Chapel of the Holy Cross in the Great Tower contains copies of 14th-century panels by Master Theodoric (the originals are in St George's Convent in Prague (➤ 67). The walls of the chapel are inlaid with over 2,000 semiprecious stones.
www.hradkarlstejn.cz

➕ 141 B2 ✉ Karlštejn ☎ 311 681 617 🕐 May, Jun, Sep daily 9–12, 12.30–5; Jul–Aug daily 9–12, 12.30–6; Apr, Oct daily 9–12, 1–4; Mar, Tue–Sun 9–12, 1–3; Nov–Dec 9–12, 1–3 ✋ Expensive 🍴 Cafés (£), restaurants (££) near by 🚆 Karlštejn from Praha-Smíchov ❓ Guided tour only

KONOPIŠTĚ

In 1887 Konopiště Castle was acquired by the heir to the Habsburg throne, Franz Ferdinand, for his Czech wife Sophie Chotek. The Archduke's abiding passion was hunting – in a career spanning 40 years he bagged more than 300,000 animals. Some of the trophies line the walls of the Great Hall. Also worth seeing is Franz Ferdinand's impressive collection of medieval arms and armour and the landscaped garden with peacocks grazing on the lawn.

www.konopiste.com

➕ 141 C3 ✉ Konopiště ☎ 317 721 366 🕐 May–Aug Tue–Sun 9–12, 1–5. Check for rest of year ✋ Expensive 🍴 Restaurant (£) 🚆 Benešov from Praha-Smíchov, then bus ❓ Guided tour only

KŘIVOKLÁT

This beautiful 13th-century castle, with its unusual 35m-high (115ft) round tower, was once the royal hunting lodge of Charles IV. Inside is the vaulted King's Hall, a Gothic chapel with a fine carved altarpiece, a dungeon once used as a prison and now home to a grim assortment of torture instruments, and the Knights' Hall, with a collection of late Gothic paintings and sculptures.

www.krivoklat.cz

➕ 141 B2 ✉ Křivoklát ☎ 313 558 440 🕐 Jul–Aug daily 9–12, 1–5; Jun Tue–Sun 9–12, 1–5; May, Sep Tue–Sun 9–12, 1–4; Apr, Oct Tue–Sun 9–12, 1–3; Mar, Nov–Dec Sat–Sun 9–12, 1–3 ✋ Moderate 🚆 Křivoklát from Praha-Smíchov, change at Beroun ❓ Guided tour only

KUTNÁ HORA

The name means 'mining mountain', and it was the discovery of large deposits of silver and copper ore in the 13th century which turned Kutná Hora overnight into one of the boom towns of Central Europe. A royal mint, founded at the beginning of the 14th century and known as the Italian Court, after Wenceslas II's Florentine advisors, produced its distinctive silver coin, *Pražské grosé*, until 1547. Visitors to the Court can see art nouveau frescoes in the Wenceslas Chapel, as well as treasures from the Gothic Town Hall, which burned down in 1770, including a brightly painted wooden statue of Christ, *Ecce Homo* (1502). The Cathedral of St Barbara was endowed by the miners and dedicated to their patron saint. Peter Parler's unusual design of three tent-roofed spires supported by a forest of flying buttresses was begun in 1388

but not completed until the end of the 15th century, when Matthias Rejsek and Benedikt Reid built the magnificent vaulted ceiling. Behind the Hrádek museum there is a medieval mine where visitors are shown the *trejv*, a horse-drawn winch used for lifting the bags of ore.

North of Kutná Hora is Sedlec, where, in the 19th century, the Cistercian ossuary was turned into a macabre work of art by František Rint. There are bone monstrances, chandeliers and even a Schwarzenberg coat of arms.

www.kutnahora.cz

✚ 141 C2 ✉ Information: Palackého náměstí 377 ☎ 327 512 378 🕔 Italian Court: Nov–Feb daily 10–3.30; Mar, Oct daily 10–4.30; Apr, Sep daily 9–5.30. St Barbara's Cathedral: Nov–Mar Tue–Sun 9–12, 2–3.30; Apr, Oct Tue–Sun

9–12,1–4; May–Sep Tue–Sun 9–5.30. Museum hrádek: Apr, Oct Tue–Sun 9–5; May–Sep Tue–Sun 9–6. Ossuary: Nov–Mar daily 9–12, 1–4; Apr–Sep daily 8–12, 1–6 🍴 Cafés (£), restaurants (££–£££) 🚆 Praha Masarykovo to Sedlec, then bus 🚌 Coach from Praha Želivského metro station ❓ Jun: international guitar competition

LIDICE

In June 1942, following the assassination of the Nazi Governor of Bohemia and Moravia, Reinhard Heydrich, this small village was one of several arbitrarily singled out for reprisal. The men were herded into a farmhouse and shot, the women and children were transported to concentration camps and the entire village was razed to the ground. The site is now a shrine with a museum – a wooden cross and a memorial mark the actual place where the men were shot and buried.

www.lidice-memorial.cz

✚ 141 B2 ✉ Památník Lidice, 273 54 Lidice ☎ 312 253 702 🕐 Apr–Sep daily 9–6, Oct–Mar daily 9–4 ✋ Inexpensive 🚌 Bus (Kladno line) from Dejvická metro station ❓ 10 Jun: memorial day

LITOMYŠL

This attractive town has one of the largest squares in the Czech Republic, with a Gothic Town Hall and Renaissance and baroque houses. 'At the Knights', built in 1540, has a superb sculpted façade: attend an art exhibition here and take a look at the panelled Renaissance ceiling. The château was built between 1568 and 1581. Its exterior is decorated with stunning sgraffiti by Šimon Vlach and the private theatre is one of the oldest in Europe. Litomyšl is also famous as the birthplace of the composer Bedřich Smetana. His apartment in the château is now a museum and music festivals take place in his honour throughout the summer.

✚ 141 D2 ✉ Information: Smetanovo náměstí 72 ☎ 461 612 161 🕐 Château: May–Aug Tue–Sun 8–12,1–5; Sep 9–12, 1–4; Apr, Oct Sat–Sun 9–12, 1–4 ✋ Inexpensive ❓ Jun–Jul: Smetana's Litomyšl (opera festival)

MĚLNÍK

Perched on a hilltop, with commanding views across the confluence of the Vltava and Labe (Elbe) rivers, is the château, Mělník's main tourist attraction. Founded in the 10th century, it originally belonged to the Bohemian royal family and was occupied by several queens, including the wives of John of Luxemburg and Charles IV, who is credited with introducing wine-making to the region. The castle passed into the hands of the Lobkowicz family early in the 17th century and they have owned it intermittently ever since. Mainly of baroque appearance, its northern wing has an impressive Renaissance arcade and loggia with sgraffito decoration, dating from 1555. The rooms have been refurbished in a variety of styles; most interesting is the Large Bedroom, which contains an early 17th-century canopied bed with a painting of the Madonna at the head. Visitors are also shown trophies and mementoes belonging to one of the château's more recent owners, Jiří Christian Lobkowicz, a talented racing driver who died tragically on a track in Berlin in 1932. There is a separate entrance charge for a tour of the 13th-century wine cellars, with tastings.

Mělník's grapes are of the Traminer and Riesling varieties.

You can also tour the Church of St Peter and Paul, built between 1480 and 1520. Its nave is roofed with splendid network and star vaulting and decorated with Renaissance and baroque paintings, including work by Karel Skřeta. The 'pewter' font is actually made of wood. The main draw here is the crypt with its fascinating charnel house, stacked from floor to ceiling with orderly rows of heaped bones – some 15,000 of them at the last count. Some of the skulls are fractured or dented – the result of bullet wounds sustained in the battles of the Thirty Years' War.
www.melnik.cz

✚ 141 C2 ✉ Turistické Informační st: náměstí Mirů ☎ 315 627 503; château: 315 622 121 ◷ Château: May, Jun, Sep Tue–Sun 9–5; Jul–Aug Tue–Sun 9–6 🖐 Moderate 🍴 Cafés and restaurants (£–£££) 🚌 Bus from Florenc coach station, Prague

PLZEŇ

Beer has been brewed in Plzeň since 1295 and the Pilsner Urquell brewery is the main attraction in this largely industrial town. The guided tour of the cellars (there are 9km/5.5 miles in all) includes a visit to the extravagantly decorated beer hall, definitely an experience not to be missed. Close by is a fascinating Museum of Brewing housed, appropriately enough, in a medieval malthouse. Plzeň's main square, náměstí Republiky, has some fine Renaissance and baroque town houses and is dominated by the Gothic Cathedral of St Bartholomew, which has the tallest steeple in the country (102m/335ft).
www.plzen-city.cz

✚ 141 B3 ✉ Information: náměstí Republiky 41 ☎ Brewery: 378 035 330. Museum: 377 235 574. Brewery visitor centre: 377 062 888 ◷ Brewery: daily 12.30 and 2pm unless booked in advance. Pivovarské Muzeum: daily 10–6 🖐 Moderate 🍴 Cafés (£), restaurants (££) 🚇 Praha Hlavní nádraží

TÁBOR

In a marvellous situation on a bluff commanding the Lužnice Valley, Tábor takes its name from the biblical mountain where Christ is said to have appeared transfigured to his disciples. After the death of Jan Hus, the Hussites transferred their allegiance to the one-eyed general Jan Žižka, who continued the struggle against the Catholics. He encamped here in 1420 and held out successfuly for four years until his death in battle. The town's attractive main square, about 20 minutes' walk from the station, is named after him and there is a statue by Josef Strachovksý.

The tower of the Church of the Transfiguration, which dates from the 16th century, offers the best views of the gabled Renaissance and classical houses and of the town itself, which is seen melting into the distance.

An exhibition in the neo-Gothic Town Hall presents an excellent account of the Hussite Movement. Don't miss the tour of the labyrinthine tunnels, 600m (1,968ft) below ground. Dating from the 15th century, they were used variously as beer cellars, as a prison for unruly women and as an escape route in time of war. When you emerge, you'll find yourself near a café where you can sit and relax. The narrow twisting streets

of the Old Town are a delight, although you may get lost from time to time. This is no accident – when the town was laid out Žižka's followers wanted to make life as confusing as possible for the enemy. A pleasant stroll along the banks of the Lužnice River leads to the Bechyňe Gate and Kotnov Castle, with its distictive round tower. Inside are some fascinating displays on medieval life in the region, with costumes, archaeological finds, farming implements and weapons. The views from the tower are a bonus.

Only 2km (1 mile) away, across beautiful countryside, is the hamlet of Klokoty, with a baroque convent and church dating from the early 18th century. The wayside shrines along the footpath mark it out as a place of Catholic pilgrimage.

On the other side of town, between Žižkovo and Tržní náměstí, is a Renaissance water tower decorated with vaulted gables and dating from 1497.

The water was pumped to the town's seven fountains from the Jordan, the oldest dam in Europe, via a system of wooden pipes.

www.tabor.cz

✚ 141 C3 ✉ Infocentrum: Žižkovo náměstí 2
☎ 381 486 230 ◷ Town Hall Museum: Apr–Oct daily 8.30–5; Nov–Mar Mon–Fri 8.30–5
✋ Inexpensive ¶ Cafés (£), restaurants (££)
✖ Praha Hlavní nádraží ❓ Sep: Tábor Meetings, a festival of parades, music and events

TEREZÍN

In 1942 the Nazis turned Terezín into a ghetto and transit camp for
Jews. More than 150,000 people ended up in extermination
camps, while a further 35,000 died of disease and starvation. At
the same time the Germans used Terezín for their perverted
propaganda purposes, persuading Red Cross visitors that this was
a flourishing cultural and commercial centre. The exhibition in the
main fortress, now restored after the flood, gives an excellent if

harrowing account of the realities of life in the camp, while across the river, in the lesser fortress, visitors can tour the barracks, workshops, isolation cells, mortuaries, execution grounds and former mass graves.

www.pamatnik-terezin.cz

✚ 141 B2 ✉ Information: Principova alej 304 ☎ 416 782 225 ◉ Apr–Oct daily 9–6; Nov–Mar daily 9–5.30 ✋ Moderate 🍴 Restaurant (£) 🚌 Coach from Praha Florenc

TŘEBOŇ

The charming spa town of Třeboň is best known for its carp ponds, which date back to the 14th century – Carp Rožmberk is still on the menu of many restaurants. Four surviving gates lead into the walled Old Town, which has at its heart a beautiful, elongated square. Dating from 1566, the Town Hall is decorated with three coats of arms: those of the town and its wealthy patrons, the Schwarzenbergs and the Rožmberks. Opposite is the 16th-century White Horse Inn, which has an unusual turreted gable. Třeboň has its own brewery and horse-drawn drays deliver Regent beer to the local hotels and restaurants. The Augustinian monastery church of St Giles dates from 1367 and contains a number of Gothic features, including a statue of the Madonna. The attractive Renaissance château is open to the public and was built in 1562 by the Rožmberk family.

✚ 141 C4 ✉ Information: Masarykovo náměstí 103 ☎ 384 721 169 ◉ Château: May–Sep Tue–Sun 9–noon, 1–5 🍴 Cafés (£), restaurants (££) 🚊 Praha Hlavní nádraží

Index

Acknowledgements

The Automobile Association would like to thank the following photographers and companies for their assistance in the preparation of this book.

Abbreviations for the picture credits are as follows – (t) top; (b) bottom; (c) centre; (l) left; (r) right; (AA) AA World Travel Library

4l Train, AA/ J Wyand; **4c** St Vitus Cathedral, AA/S McBride; **4r** Charles Bridge, AA/S McBride; **5l** Cesky Krumlov, AA/J Wyand; **5c** View from Letna, AA/J Smith; **5r** Waldstein Palace, AA/C Sawyer; **6/7** Train, AA/J Wyand; **10** Czech Symphony Orchestra, AA/J Wyand; **11** Market in Old Town Square, AA/S McBride; **12** Aeroplane, Digitalvision; **12/13** Tancici dum, AA/J Smith; **14/15** Marksmen's Island, AA/J Smith; **16** Telephone booths, AA/S McBride; **18** Post box, AA/J Smith; **20/21** St Vitus Cathedral, AA/S McBride; **22/23** Church of St Nicholas, AA/T Souter; **23** View from Church of St Nicholas, AA/S McBride; **24** Franz Kafka Memorial Statue, AA/J Smith; **24/25** Market in Jewish Quarter, AA/S McBride; **25** Old Jewish Cemetery, AA/S McBride; **26cl** St Vitus Cathedral, AA/S McBride; **26bl** Sculpture, St Vitus Cathedral, AA/T Souter; **27t** St Vitus Cathedral at night, AA; **27b** Alfons Mucha window, St Vitus Cathedral, AA/J Wyand; **28** Loreta Church, AA/S McBride; **28/29** Loreta Church, AA/S McBride; **30tr** Prague Castle Guard, AA/J Smith; **30cr** Castle Gardens, AA/C Sawyer; **30/31** Prague Castle, AA/J Smith; **31tl** Chapel of the Holy Cross in Prague Castle, AA/C Sawyer; **32** Astronomical Clock, AA/C Sawyer; **33** Astronomical Clock, AA/S McBride; **34/35** National Gallery, AA/J Smith; **36** Strahov Gospel, Strahov Monastery, AA/S McBride; **36/37** Philosophical Hall, Strahov Monastery, AA/S McBride; **37** Strahov Monastery, AA/S McBride; **38/39** Wenceslas Square, AA/S McBride; **39** Wenceslas Square building, AA/S McBride; **40** Trade Fair Palace, AA/J Smith; **40/41** Atrium, Trade Fair Palace, AA/J Smith; **42/43** Busker on Charles Bridge, AA/S McBride; **45** Old Town Square, AA/J Smith; **46** Bethlehem Chapel, AA/T Souter; **47cr** Black Madonna House, AA/J Smith; **48br** Statue, Black Madonna House, AA/C Sawyer; **49** Stone Bell House, Old Town Square, AA/J Wyand; **50** Charles Bridge, AA/J Wyand; **51** Carolinum, AA/C Sawyer; **52** Library Hall, Klementinum, AA/J Smith; **53** Courtyard, Klementinum, AA/J Smith; **54** Charles IV Statue, Knights of the Cross Square, AA/S McBride; **54/55** Church of the Holy Saviour, AA/S McBride; **56b** Bedrich Smetana Statue, AA/J Wyand; **56/57** Bedrich Smetana Museum, AA/S McBride; **58** Old Town Square; AA/S McBride; **58/59** Jan Hus Monument, AA/J Wyand; **59** Estates Theatre, AA/J Wyand; **60t** Ungelt, AA/J Smith; **60b** Wine shop, Ungelt, AA/J Smith; **61** St George's Convent, AA/J Smith; **62** Mozart Museum, AA/J Wyand; **63t** Battle of the White Mountain Memorial, AA/J Wyand; **63b** Brevnov Monastery, AA/J Wyand; **64** Cernin Palace, AA/J Wyand; **65t** Building detail, Hradcany Square, AA/J Wyand; **65b** Schwartzenberg Palace, Hradcany Square, AA/C Sawyer; **66** Basilica of St George, AA/J Wyand; **67** St George's Convent, AA/J Smith; **68** Church of Our Lady of Victory, AA/T Souter; **68/69** View from Hradcany District, AA/C Sawyer; **70b** Singing Fountain, Royal Gardens, AA/S McBride; **70/71** Royal Gardens, AA/S McBride; **71** Lapidarium, AA/C Sawyer; **72/73** John Lennon Wall, AA/J Wyand; **73** Mala Strana Square, AA/S McBride; **74** National Technical Museum, AA/J Wyand; **74/75** Nerudova, AA/J Wyand; **77** Church of St Lawrence, AA/J Wyand; **78** Waterwheel, Certovka AA/S McBride; **78/79** View over Malostranke Namesti, AA/S McBride; **80** Troja Chateau AA/C Sawyer; **81** Waldstein Gardens, AA/C Sawyer; **82** Exhibition Hall, AA/C Sawyer; **83** Golden Lane, AA/S McBride; **84** Old-New Synagogue, AA/S McBride; **85t** St Agnes's Convent, AA/J Smith; **85b** Altarpiece in St Agnes's Convent, AA/J Smith; **86** Franz Kafky Plaque, AA/J Wyand; **86/87** Old Jewish Cemetery, AA/S McBride; **89** Maiselova Synagoga, AA/J Smith; **90** Old Jewish Cemetery, AA/T Souter; **91** Drawings from Terezin, Pinkas Synagogue, AA/J Smith/Jewish Museum, Prague; **92** Rudolfinum, AA/S McBride; **93** Old-New Synagogue, AA/J Wyand; **94** Old Jewish Cemetery, AA/T Souter; **95** Church of St Cyril and St Methodius, AA/J Smith; **96** Church of Our Lady of the Snows, AA/J Wyand; **97** Memorial, Church of St Cyril and St Methodius, AA/C Sawyer; **98/99** Painting, 'Old Town Square in Winter', City Museum, AA/J/Smith; **99** Stalin Bust, Museum of Communism, AA/J Smith; **101** National Theatre, AA/J Smith; **102/103** National Museum, AA/J Wyand; **103** Municipal House, AA/S McBride; **105** Powder Tower, AA/C Sawyer; **106** Church of St Peter and St Paul, AA/C Sawyer; **107** Europa Hotel, AA/J Wyand; **108/109** Cesky Krumlov, AA/J Wyand; **111** Brno, AA/J Wyand; **112/113** Church of St Peter and St Paul, AA/J Wyand; **113** Melnik Town Hall, AA/J Wyand; **115** Cesky Krumlov, AA/J Wyand; **116** Hradec Kralove, AA/J Wyand; **116/117c** Karlovy Vary, AA/J Wyand; **118/119** Karlstejn Castle, AA/C Sawyer; **120** Vlassky Dvur in Kutna Hora, AA/J Wyand; **122** Melnik Town Hall, AA/J Wyand; **123** Brewery, Plzen AA/J Wyand; **124/125** Jan Zizka statue, Tabor, AA/J Wyand; **126/127** Terezin, AA/J Wyand.

Every effort has been made to trace the copyright holders, and we apologise in advance for any accidental errors. We would be happy to apply the corrections in the following edition of this publication.

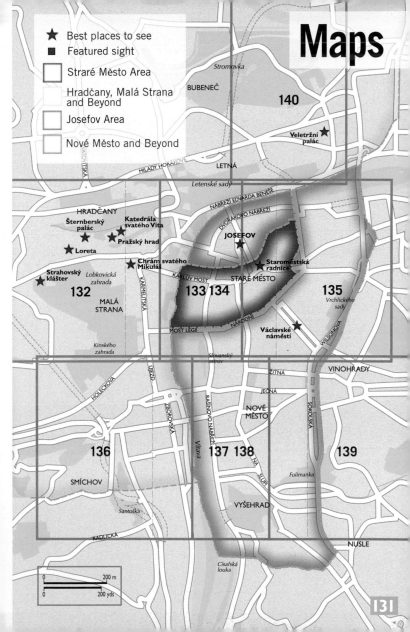

Maps

- ★ Best places to see
- ■ Featured sight
- ☐ Straré Město Area
- ☐ Hradčany, Malá Strana and Beyond
- ☐ Josefov Area
- ☐ Nové Město and Beyond

Stromovka

BUBENEČ

140

Veletržní palác ★

ŠVATOPLUKOVA

MILADY HORÁKOVÉ

LETNÁ

Letenské sady

NÁBŘEŽÍ EDVARDA BENEŠE

HRADČANY

DVOŘÁKOVO NÁBŘEŽÍ

Šternberský palác

Katedrála svatého Víta

JOSEFOV ★

Loreta ★

Pražský hrad ■

★ Staroměstská radnice

Strahovský klášter ★

Chrám svatého Mikuláš ■

Lobkovická zahrada

KARMELITSKÁ

KARLŮV MOST

STARÉ MĚSTO

135

132

MALÁ STRANA

Vrchlického sady

MOST LEGIÍ

NÁRODNÍ

133 134

Kinského zahrada

Václavské náměstí ★

WILSONOVA

Slovanský ostrov

ŽITNÁ

VINOHRADY

JEČNÁ

ÚJEZD

HOLEČKOVA

ZBOROVSKÁ

RAŠÍNOVO NÁBŘEŽÍ

NOVÉ MĚSTO

SOKOLSKÁ

136

Vltava

137 138

NA SLUPI

Folimanka

139

SMÍCHOV

Santoška

VYŠEHRAD

RADLICKÁ

NUSLE

Císařská louka

| 0 | 200 m |
| 0 | 200 yds |

131

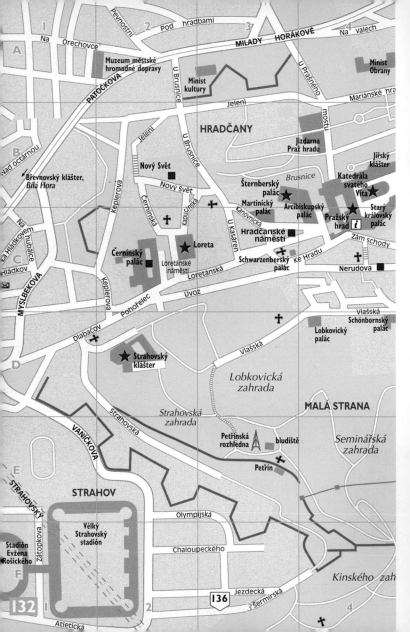

Na Orechovce
Pevnostní
Pod hradbami
MILADY HORÁKOVÉ
Na valech

A

Muzeum městské hromadné dopravy
Minist kultury
PATOČKOVA
U Brusnice
Minist Obrany
U Prašného
Mariánské hra

Jeleni

HRADČANY

Nad octárnou
Jeleni
U Brusnice
Jizdárna Praž hradu
mostu
Jiřský klášter

B

Nový Svět
Keplerova
Nový svět
Černínská
Kanovnická
Brusnice
Šternberský palác ★
Martinický palác
Arcibiskupský palác
Katedrála svatého Víta ★
Pražský hrad ⓘ
Starý královský palác ★

Na hubálkovem
Nad Hládkovem
Hládkov
Loreta ★
Černínský palác
Loretánské náměstí
U Kasáren
Hradčanské náměstí
Schwarzenberský palác
Loretánská
Ke Hradu
Zám schody
Nerudova

C

MYSLBEKOVA
Dlabačov
Keplerova
Pohořelec
Úvoz
Vlašská
Lobkovický palác
Schönbornský palác

D

Strahovský klášter ★
Strahovská
Strahovská zahrada
Lobkovická zahrada
Vlašská
MALÁ STRANA

VANÍČKOVA
Strahovská zahrada
Petřínská rozhledna
bludiště
Petřín
Seminářská zahrada

E

STRAHOVSKÝ
STRAHOV
Zátopkova
Velký Strahovský stadión
Olympijská

Stadión Evžena Rošického
Chaloupeckého

F

Kinského zah
Jezdecká
Šermířská
Atletická

⬡ 136

132

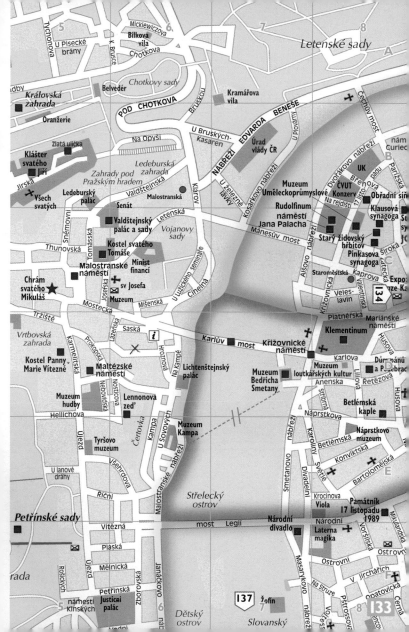

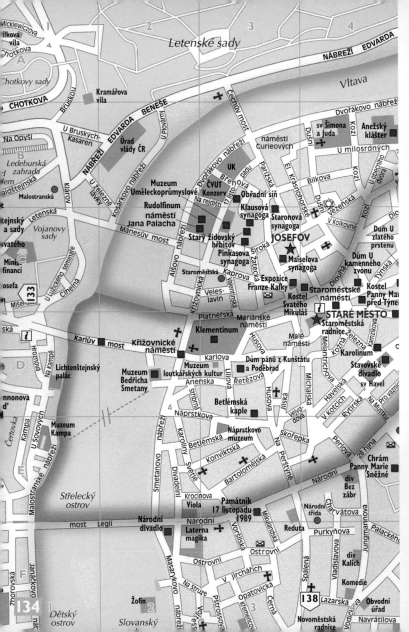

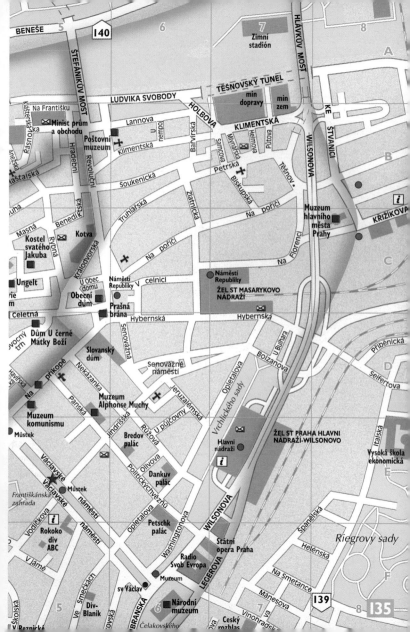

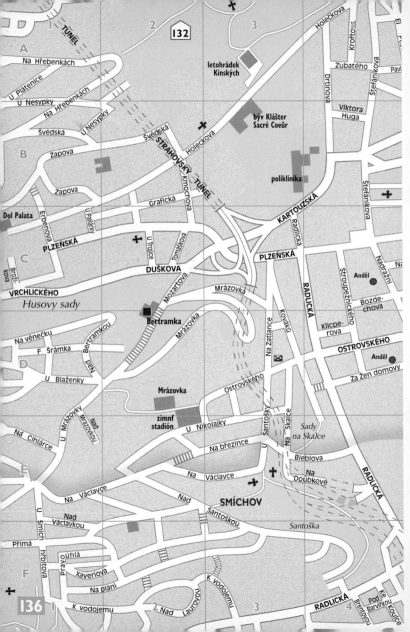

letohrádek Kinských

býv Klášter Sacré Coeûr

poliklinika

Na Hřebenkách

U Plátenice

U Nesypky

Na Hřebenkách

Švédská

U Nesypky

Švédská

Zapova

Zapova

STRAHOVSKÝ TUNEL

Holečkova

Kmochova

Grafická

Erbenova

Dol Palata

U Palárky

PLZEŇSKÁ

KARTOUZSKÁ

Radlická

Brožíkova

U Trojice

Tůmovka

Tůmovka

DUŠKOVA

PLZEŇSKÁ

VRCHLICKÉHO

Husovy sady

Mrázovka

RADLICKÁ

Anděl

Stroupežnického

Nádražní

Na věnečku

Mozartova

Mrázovka

Na Zatlance

Kováků

Klicperova

Bozdě-chova

OSTROVSKÉHO

F. Šrámka

Bertramkou

Bertramka

Mrázovka

Anděl

PLZEŇ

U Blaženky

Mrázovka

Ostrovského

Za Ženy domovy

Na Cihlárce

U Mrázovky

Nad Mrázovkou

Mrázovka

zimní stadión

U Nikolajky

Na Skalce

Santošky

U

Sady na Skalce

Na březince

Bieblova

Na Doubkové

RADLICKÁ

Na Václavce

Na Václavce

Nad Santoškou

SMÍCHOV

Santoška

U Smích

Nad Václavkou

Přímá

Pravoúhlá

Xaveriova

Na pláni

hřbitova

K vodojemu

K vodojemu

Nad Laurovou

K vodojemu

RADLICKÁ

Pod Barvírkou

Ke Koulce

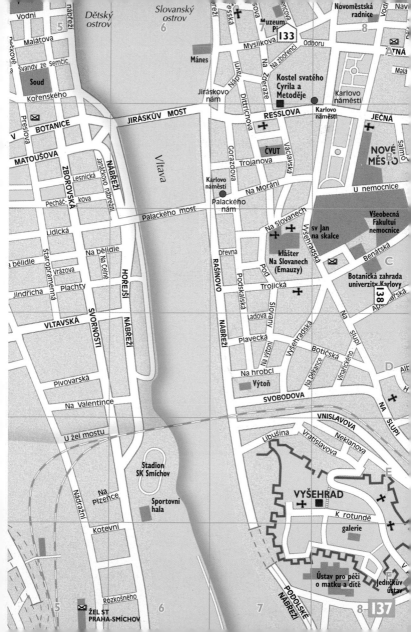

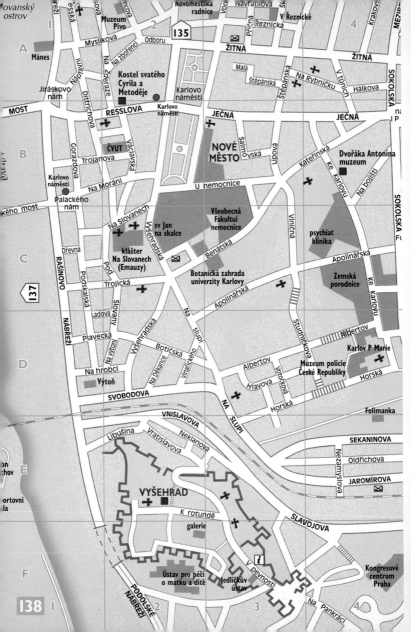

Slovanský ostrov

Muzeum Pivo

Novoměstská radnice

Navrátilova

V Řeznické

Řeznická

Příčná

A

Myslíkova

Odboru

135

ŽITNÁ

ŽITNÁ

SOKOLSKÁ

Mánes

Na zbořenci

Malá

Na Rybníčku

V tůních

Štěpánská

Na zderaze

Jiráskovo nám

Dittrichova

Kostel svatého Cyrila a Metoděje

Karlovo náměstí

Štěpánská

Hálkova

MOST

RESSLOVA

Karlovo náměstí

JEČNÁ

JEČNÁ

na P

B

Gorazdova

Trojanova

ČVUT

Václavská

NOVÉ MĚSTO

Salmovská

Lipová

Kateřinská

Ke Karlovu

Na bojišti

Dvořáka Antonína muzeum

SOKOLSKÁ

Karlovo náměstí

Na Moráni

U nemocnice

Palackého nám

kého most

Na Slovanech

sv Jan na skalce

Vyšehradská

Všeobecná Fakultuí nemocnice

Vinična

psychiat klinika

Fu

C

RAŠÍNOVO

Dřevná

Pod

Benátská

Apolinářská

Ke Karlovu

137

Podskalská

klášter Na Slovanech (Emauzy)

Botanická zahrada univerzity Karlovy

Zemská porodnice

Trojická

Ladova

Slovany

Na slupi

Apolinářská

Studničkova

Albertov

Karlov P Marie

D

NÁBŘEŽÍ

Plavecká

Na výtoni

Vyšehradská

Botičská

Vnislavova

Albertov

Vodičkova

Hlavova

Muzeum policie České Republiky

Horská

Na Děkance

NA SLUPI

Horská

Na hrobci

Výtoň

SVOBODOVA

VNISLAVOVA

Folimanka

Libušina

Vratislavova

Neklanova

SEKANINOVA

E

on chov

Vyšehradská

Nezamyslova

Oldřichova

JAROMÍROVA

ortovní la

VYŠEHRAD

SLAVOJOVA

K rotundě

galerie

F

Ústav pro péči o matku a dítě

Jedličkův ústav

i

V pevnosti

Kongresové centrum Praha

PODOLSKÉ NÁBŘEŽÍ

Na Pankráci

2

3

4

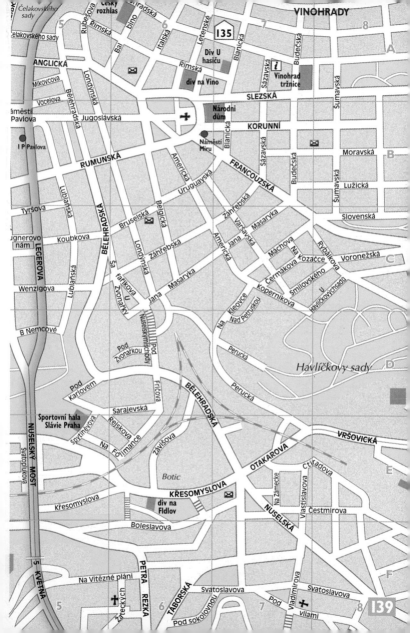

VINOHRADY

Čelakovského sady
Čelakovského sady

Český rozhlas

Rubešova
Římská
Blodkova
Italská
Letenská
Blanická
Budečská
Šumavská

135

Div U hasiču

Anglická

Mikovcova
Vocelova
Londýnská
Bělehradská
Jugoslávská

div na Vino

i

Vinohrad tržnice

SLEZSKÁ

náměstí
Pavlova

I P Pavlova

Národní
dům

KORUNNÍ

Moravská

RUMUNSKÁ

Náměstí
Míru

Americká

Blanická

Sázavská
Budečská
Šumavská
Lužická

FRANCOUZSKÁ

Uruguayská

Slovenská

Tyršova
Lublaňská

BĚLEHRADSKÁ

Bruselská
Belgická
Londýnská
Záhřebská

Žitná
Fartíkova

Zvonařky

Záhřebská
Varšavská
Masaryka

Jana
Masaryka

Americká

Máchova
Na Kozáčce
Rybalkova
Voronežská

Čermákova
Smilovského

Koubkova

Jana Masaryka

Kopernikova

U
Havlíčkových sadů

Lublaňská

Wenzigova

Na Kleovce
Nad Petruskou

B Němcové

Pod
Zvonařkou

Nuselským schody

Perucká

Havlíčkovy sady

LEGEROVA

Pod
Karlovem

Fričova

BĚLEHRADSKÁ

Perucká

Sportovní hala
Slávie Praha

Sarajevská
Rejskova

VRŠOVICKÁ

Sportovní
Na Folimance

Závišova

OTAKAROVA

Ctíradova

NUSELSKÝ MOST

Svatoplukova

Botic

KŘESOMYSLOVA

Na Zámecké

Vlastislavova

Čestmírova

div na
Fidlov

NUSELSKÁ

Křesomyslova

Boleslavova

5 KVĚTNA

Na Vitězné pláni

Žateckých

PETRA
REZKA

TÁBORSKÁ

Svatoslavova

Pod sokolovnou

Pod
vilami

Vladimírova

svatoslavova

139

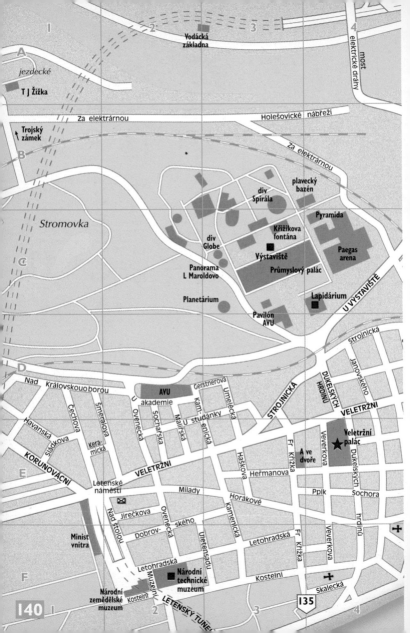

Vodácká
základna

A

jezdecké

T J Žižka

Za elektrárnou
Holešovické nábřeží

↑ Trojský
zámek

za elektrárnou

B

Stromovka

div
Spirála

plavecký
bazén

Pyramida

Křižíkova
fontána

div
Globe

Výstaviště

**Paegas
arena**

C

Panorama
L Maroldovo

Průmyslový palác

Planetárium

Lapidárium

U VÝSTAVIŠTĚ

Pavilón
AVU

Strojnická

D

Nad   Královskouoborou

AVU
akademie

Čerstnerova

Umělecká

Kam...

STROJNICKÁ

DUKELSKÝCH
HRDINŮ

Janovského

VELETRŽNÍ

U Ovenecká

Sochařská

Malířská

U studánky

...enická

Fr
Křížka

Veverkova

**Veletržní
palác**

Havanská

Čechova

Šmeralova

Kera-
mická

A ve
dvoře

Dukelských

KORUNOVAČNI

VELETRŽNÍ

Haškova

Heřmanova

Pplk

Sochora

Letenské
náměstí

Milady

Horákové

hrdinů

✉

Jirečkova

Ovenecká

-ského

Kamenická

Fr
Křížka

Veverkova

Minist
vnitra

Nad štolou

Dobrov-

Ovenecká

Uletensadu

Letohradská

Kostelni

Letohradská

Muzejní

**Národní
technické
muzeum**

Kostelni

skalecká

F

Národní
zemědělské
muzeum

Kostelni

LETENSKÝ TUNE...

135

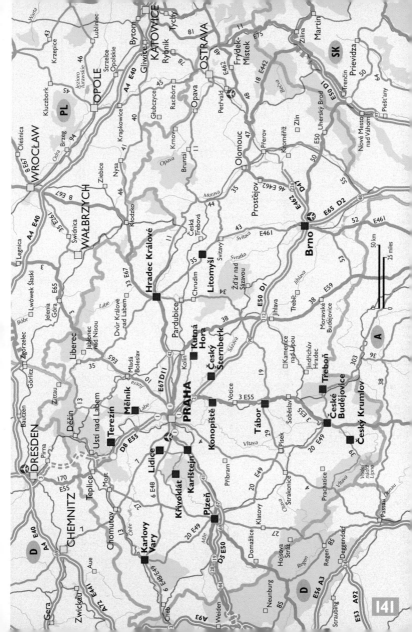

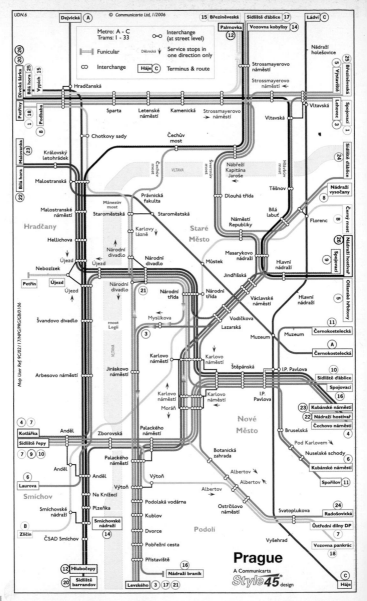

Prague

A Communicarta Style45 design